Bitch Up!

Expect More, Get More

A Woman's Survival Guide to Keeping Her Power and Sanity After a Breakup

Written By **Leslie Braswell**

Other Books by Leslie Braswell

Ignore the Guy, Get the Guy
The Art of No Contact
A Woman's Survival Guide to Mastering a Breakup and Taking Back Her Power

How to Be the Girl Who Gets the Guy
How Confident and Self-Assured Women Handle Dating with Class and Sass

Printed by Kindle Direct Publishing
An Amazon.com Company

Available from Amazon.com and other bookstores
Also Available on Kindle and other devices

Cover designed by 99 Designs

Leslie Braswell

Printed in the United States of America

First Printing: 2018
CreateSpace

ISBN – 13: 978-0-692-05813-8

.

Contents

Bitch Up!

Elizabeth Taylor once said, "Pour yourself a drink, put on some lipstick, and pull yourself together." *"Bitch Up!"* in this title means just that, "Pull yourself together and get on with it." It's used to give women who are habitual "man-pleasers" the courage, incentive, and motivation they need to grow a backbone, have confidence, and develop a new sense of self. The empowerment to strive to be a confident, self-assured woman who can easily stand up for herself when she is not receiving the best a man has to offer. And the courage to expect more and get more.

Let's get started!

Chapter 1
Why No Contact is Crucial

∞ ∞ ∞

"Silence is the sleep that nourishes wisdom." --

FRANCIS BACON

*H*ave you ever heard a man talk about his crazy ex? *Maybe you've been called the crazy ex.* Have you ever had a breakdown after a breakup? Have you ever cried, begged and bargained for a man to take you back? Refused to let go? If so, learning to master the art of *No Contact* is not only vital to a breakup you are currently dealing with, but to any future relationship you have. No contact is used to allow you to exit a relationship, whether amicable or not, with your pride, dignity, and sanity intact. Calm and composed is how one needs to appear, but when facing the realism of a breakup, it is anything but how one comes across.

A broken heart is hell. Actual, physical, hell. There is no statute of limitations on a broken heart. There is no way of placing a deadline on when you *should* start feeling better. And you shouldn't give yourself one. It takes time to heal and move on. Right now, you feel as if you will never be happy again. You can feel the ache in your heart. Can I fast forward a bit and tell you something that won't make you feel any better right now, but it is true? I promise, in time, you will feel better if you take baby steps to move forward. A broken heart is only temporary. What I want to do is kickstart your recovery and expedite the process so you can move on to a better life, faster. With no contact, you can accomplish this goal.

If you're one of the few women who can politely step aside after being blindsided by a breakup, bravo, good for you! If, on the other hand, you're one of the many women who fall to pieces, when a relationship doesn't go your way, this book was written with you in mind. If you want a fighting chance to reverse a breakup and get the respect and love you deserve, the no contact rule is definitely right for you. Remember, how you handle yourself initially after a breakup is what ultimately determines the outcome.

What is your plan? What are you hoping for? To get Mr. Ex back? Do you want to move on completely? Do you want to stop feeling so alone? Do you want to create a fantastic new life? What if I tell you to accomplish a reconciliation with Mr. Ex, to stop feeling lonely, or to create an incredible new life all require the same steps.

For purposes of this book, the No Contact Rule is not used to be mean, cold-hearted, hurtful, or manipulative. Instead, the no contact rule is to advance you to a place of happiness and peace. Whether you are a die-hard rules girl, or don't give a damn about following any rules, I hope by the conclusion of this book you have a better understanding of what it takes to navigate your way through the breakup process to come through better, stronger and happier.

When used the right way, no contact brings peace of mind. It's used to give you the wakeup call needed to make yourself a priority. It's used to put you on the fast track to the healing process. It's used to clear your mind of uncertainties. It's used to keep you as a contender to one day walk down the aisle with the love of your life. It's about being able to move on with your head held high, no regrets, and no charges filed with the local police. It's about creating the life you want, whether that means having a man in your life, or being perfectly happy and content on your own. It's used to help find harmony during your most trying days. The no contact rule is best used as a smokescreen to hide the fact you may be falling apart on the inside, going a little crazy, and acting a little irrational. Most importantly, no contact is implemented to give a man who has broken your heart the wake-up call he desperately needs.

Using no contact alone can't get your ex back. However, getting back to the woman he fell in love with (only better), often works impeccably. Man-pleasers often lose themselves in a relationship. Unintentionally, they focus like a laser, taking drastic measures to make a man happy while shifting the focus from themselves. How many times did you want to do one thing but *went along to get along* just to keep him happy? Did you cater to him by putting your life on the back burner while running in circles to make sure his needs were met? Have you ever bit your tongue for fear of saying something that would rock the relationship boat?

This is what the Dalai Lama, the foremost spiritual leader of Buddhism, wisely counseled about silence. He said, "Sometimes one creates a dynamic impression by saying something, and sometimes one creates as significant an impression by remaining silent." Recognizing you need to begin no contact is the first step to taking back your power and control. Being strong enough to implement no contact is a real testament to willpower, patience, determination, discipline, and restraint. Make up your mind right now, you are strong enough to do this to get the love and respect you deserve.

Right after a breakup, you may think it's smart to fire off a text message, or thirty more will make you feel better. Some women drop down on all fours trying to "plead their case" to convince him to change his mind. Unfortunately, this is when they lose the battle of the breakup from the start. Men anticipate the tears to flow like a waterfall. He expects you to declare (through sniffles and sobs), "I won't ever be able to find anyone like you!" and, "How can I live without you?" Instead, a smart woman uses silence to conceal her emotions. By going silent, she throws a monkey wrench into his system by doing the unexpected. A clever woman may be falling apart on the inside, but on the outside, she never looked better.

When you are heartbroken, hurt, baffled, sad, numb, and infuriated all at the same time, you may feel rejected and worthless. These emotions are entirely normal, but when combined, they can cause illogical, irrational feelings to flood through you like tidal waves slamming into a seawall. The feelings you are experiencing are perfectly normal immediately after a man breaks your heart into a million pieces. Dealing with so many raw emotions all at once can bring out a woman's worst fears and behavior. So, while there may be specific actions you *want* to take that may seem perfectly rational and may even bring you comfort if acted upon, may land you forever classified as the "crazy one." To prevent him from thinking you're a few clowns short of a circus, you must exercise "attitude control." Having attitude control requires being able to recognize some urges you may have, if acted upon, can be irreparable and irreversible. When you spiral out of control, demeaning yourself, the faster you fall from grace.

Rather than obsessing about ways to contact Mr. Ex, rewire your brain to think about ways to enhance your life for the better. To keep your mind from spinning out of control, focus on your health, envision the life you want, excelling at work, or taking on a new project. You've heard the old saying, "Idle hands are the devil's

6

workshop." The same can be true of an idle mind after a split. If you don't have something to occupy your time, you'll spend too much time overanalyzing every single detail of what went wrong.

Many women pose the question, "How can I stop thinking about Mr. Ex when he is all I think about?" My answer is: Just stop and redirect your attention. I know you're rolling your eyes, but I can assure you that over time you can train your mind to refocus your attention. When you begin to obsessively overthink, you must force yourself to get up and busy. There will be days when you don't want to get out of bed. *Get out of bed anyway.* There will be days when you don't want to go to work. *Go through the motions and go to work anyway.* There will be times you don't want to go out with friends and would rather stay home. *Go out with friends anyway.* Even if your heart isn't in it, just go through the motions. Train yourself to divert your attention when thoughts creep into your mind. Try taking a 15-minute walk, watch a new television series, go shopping, read a book, cook a recipe you've wanted to try, call the friends you've neglected, get dolled up and go out with your girlfriends for a night on the town. You get the idea, don't you? If you refocus your attention while navigating through the first thirty days, I can assure you it will get easier as time passes.

There will be a time when he calls (because they always do) to tie up loose ends. When he does reach out, be indifferent, yet friendly. Make him feel at ease, but don't gush over him. Don't seem sad, pathetic, and depressed either. Remember, a man will not call if he feels as if he needs to book a therapy session after having a conversation. Don't nag, bitch, whine, or go postal. Your job is to make communication easy by being light, breezy, and uncomplicated. Respond with kindness and make it a pleasant experience. By keeping it upbeat, he is left with the impression you will be easy to talk to the next time he gets the urge to call.

If you act as if you could care less about the outcome of the breakup because you don't want Mr. Ex to see your disappointment, it could backfire. He may believe that because you don't care, he shouldn't either. By appearing too strong, you could make matters worse. How you win is by showing you are *stirred*, not shaken. By letting go of hurt feelings because he acted in a certain way or made a decision that left you bewildered and wounded, you demonstrate you can move forward by leaving the past in the past. Find a way to express in a calm, mature way you are disappointed, perhaps even devastated. That you really want to make your relationship work, but more than anything, *you* want to be happy again.

If Mr. Ex reciprocates the same feelings, this is excellent news. You are off to a terrific start. You both want to work in a joint effort to find resolutions to problems you both are facing. It demonstrates you can handle trying times maturely. However, if he expresses no desire to make an effort on his own to fix what is broken, take a giant step back.

Six Breakup Rules to Always Live by

1. Hide Your Crazy Side: Have you gotten a little drunk and called Mr. Ex in the middle of the night? Stayed up all night stalking his social media sites, because hey, he could post a status update at any time? And who in the hell is that girl Heather who 'Liked' his profile picture? Have you stalked his friend's social media accounts? Hacked his email? Driven by his house in the wee hours of the morning to see if another car is parked outside his house? Called his number just to hang up? Did you run into him by "happenstance" at the gym he frequents? The list could go on, but you get my point.

Bitch Up!

This desperate behavior may seem pathetic and over the top, but it's precisely what some women reduce themselves to after a bad breakup. If you have done or even contemplated doing any of the above obsessive behavior, now is the time to calm down and take a step back. It's just a breakup. It's not the end of the world. Don't be ashamed if you have gotten a little fixated and gone overboard. You can't unscramble an egg, but you can stop. Many women who are scared begin to act desperate, which ruins a chance of Mr. Ex changing his mind. If you're going to win him back, you must have the power to remain calm. A real test of value is how a woman holds up when things get tough.

To stop your overactive imagination, avoid spying on his social media. Don't hack into his email. And don't track his every move like a GPS. You and only you can control your actions at this time. One day you will want to be able to look Mr. Ex in the eyes and have a conversation. You may feel out of control because everything seems to be falling apart. What is vital is you get through this stretch without drastic displays of desperation. When your mind spirals out of control, apply the brakes. For your emotional well-being, adopt the mindset, "ignorance is bliss." What you don't know won't hurt you. Possess self-control, and do nothing that diminishes your self-worth.

2. Never Seek Closure: When a relationship ends, it may be essential for you to have closure. For women, it's important they understand why it ended? They need closure to bring clarity. If you are one of the lucky ones who know why a romantic relationship ended, you won't seek closure because you already have it. If, on the other hand, you were blindsided, you may have so many unanswered questions running through your mind, you may think your brain will explode. You just want to talk, you know, have a simple conversation. You want to know what you did to make Mr. Ex never, ever want to talk to you again? More importantly, you want validation that you are, at the very least, worth a decent 'Goodbye.' You have questions, and you want him to provide you with answers. Immediately.

Before you send the first or fifteenth text, practice restraint and wait it out. Waiting twenty-four hours before firing off a text message the length of a book gives you plenty of time to think it through carefully. Remember, you can't unring a bell. After a split, a man has no desire to speak with you and frankly doesn't understand your need to do so. Chances are he has set your ringtone to the emergency alert warning sound, so he doesn't accidentally answer your call. Right now, he'd rather negotiate with a used car salesman than talk about his feelings.

When seeking closure, you're on a quest for a perfectly brilliant explanation to make you feel better. You are trying to obtain something you will never receive. The perfect answer will never come. Chances are, Mr. Ex is at a loss for words and could not accurately articulate his feelings if his life depended on it. Men have a hard time verbalizing their feelings on a good day, so odds of him acing it on a bad day are slim to none. It doesn't matter if you know he's capable of having a conversation, just understand he doesn't want to have a conversation with you. Right now, the only course of action you have is to accept Mr. Ex's decision and walk away. For whatever reason, he doesn't want to be in a relationship with you. It doesn't mean you aren't beautiful, kind, smart, funny, or a kick-ass woman. It just means he has different needs you can't provide right now.

Real power comes when you can accept the breakup for what it is and move on without closure. What advances you to a happy place in life is when you accept what you can't control. You may not have the closure you want but understand you don't need it. Maybe the outcome wasn't what you wanted. Instead of wasting your time over-analyzing something you may never understand, accept it. Recognize the heartache you feel now is temporary.

3. Refrain from Expressing Your Love or Anger: With so many avenues of communication, you may have done what many women do and go a bit crazy and fired off twenty-three text messages over a three-minute time frame. Avoid making the mistake of sending another one explaining, justifying, or defending your actions. You're in pain. Your heart is hurting. Expressing your feelings, regardless of what method you use, is a way to show your sadness, and in a small way, gives you comfort. Sending yet one more message relays that you now wish to correct your erratic behavior by sending what he will view as just one more annoying message.

If he does accept your call and gets an ass-chewing the minute he answers, he will never call back. If you have talked about the relationship to death, understand he was mentally finished before you knew what happened. Keep in mind a man would rather eat a bar of soap than listen to a nagging woman. When he does reach out to you, keep it light and enjoyable.

If you pull yourself together and give him space, he'll eventually forget about your erratic behavior and remember the good times. A man's brain can only retain so much for so long. Think about a Monday Night football game. Instant replay was created so a man could remember. If you stop feeding him the craziness (the instant replay), he will eventually forget the madness. No further explanation is needed or required. If a man truly loves you, he won't stop loving you even if your actions cast you, temporarily, in an unfavorable light.

4. Don't Compete with other Women: If there is another woman in the picture, your first feeling may be that of jealousy. Your investigation skills kick in, and before you know it, you're in the full-blown undercover mode to find out everything there is to know about the new woman. You may start comparing yourself to her, and depending on the type of woman she is, it may make you feel good or terrible. Either way, the last thing you want to do is compare yourself to anyone because, at the end of the day, it just doesn't matter. What matters is you continue to stay focused and put your best self forward.

Do you remember when Prince Charles confessed in a televised interview, he had an affair with the now Duchess of Cornwall, Camilla Parker-Bowles? It was the ultimate slap in the face to Princess Diana. It was reported she was humiliated, heartbroken, and felt betrayed. How easy it would have been for her to hide behind the gates of Kensington Palace and have a pity party for one. Instead of retreating, she got up, got dressed, and held her head high as she stepped out in what is now famously referred to as the "Little Black Revenge Dress." This move alone revealed her grit. She showed Prince Charles what he was missing and left everyone scratching their heads, asking, "What in the hell is the Prince thinking?" *Mission accomplished.*

Regardless of how hard it is on you when an ex begins to date again, you must find a way to move on with your life. Over analyzing the other woman will do nothing but eat away at your soul. You may think she has everything, but she doesn't. She may have the same problems you do. Chances are she may be jealous of you, resent you, and wishes she could be you. Instead of remembering all the good in Mr. Ex, think about the annoying little things he did that drove you crazy. No man is one-hundred percent perfect so, focus your mind on his imperfections. Take comfort in knowing she is now dealing with the irritating habits that once drove you crazy.

In the end, it's better to walk away with your head held high and dignity intact rather than to make a fool of yourself over a man who is simply not deserving of a fantastic woman like you. You deserve a man who will make you his top priority.

5. Don't Beg, Plead, or Bargain: Few behaviors depreciate a woman's value more than groveling for a do-over. Some women justify it in their minds by believing if a man could only see how much he means to her, how badly she wants him, it would change his mind forever, and they could just forget this whole little misunderstanding ever happened. *Wrong.* Desperation robs the most beautiful women in the world of the one quality men find so attractive; Self-respect.

Groveling, begging, and offering everything you have are bargaining chips a woman should never use while trying to *convince* Mr. Ex to stay. A high-value woman won't try to convince at all. She doesn't want anyone to stay where they don't want to be. If a man's decision has been made to leave, tell him you would like to find a way to make it work, but let your actions reflect you won't degrade yourself in the process. To stroke his ego one last time, tell him, "You are the best man I've dated *so far.*" This tells him, 'there is more to come.' And then focus on seeking ways to elevate your life to the next level. When you don't have a breakdown because of a breakup, at least a public one, your pride and integrity remain unscathed. When you don't crawl on all fours trying to persuade a man to stay, when you don't call hysterically, begging for one more chance, it leaves his ego in a state of confusion. And the one thing a man can't ignore is his ego because it follows him around like a lost puppy. If you can adopt an 'Oh well' approach, you win.

Don't allow your first instinct to fix what's broken overpower your emotions. Understand, even though it's hard, even though it's frustrating, right now, doing nothing is the best course of action. Fight the urge to kick it into high gear with efforts trying to win back Mr. Ex.

6. Don't fake an illness for sympathy: Just don't do it.

Ten Simple Reasons to Never Beg

1. Begging makes Mr. Ex lose respect for you.
2. Begging makes you appear desperate.
3. Begging makes you look weak.
4. Begging lowers your self-value.
5. Begging is demeaning.
6. Begging is degrading.
7. Begging diminishes your self-worth
8. Begging robs you of self-confidence.
9. Begging robs you of self-esteem.
10. Begging will not get the results you want.

If you are any of the above, I can almost guarantee there will not be a reunion with Mr. Ex. Why? Because men don't fall in love with desperate women, nor do they bend down on one knee and ask for their hand in marriage. Men look for a strong woman who has a "When the going gets tough, the tough get going," mentality. They want a strong woman who can take care of her life. One who doesn't let a man make her messy.

Some women go through life, preparing for the perfect man to come along. They envision a life of love and how happy they will be once they meet Mr. Right without giving a single thought as to how they would handle it if the perfect man walks out the door. The woman who gets Mr. Ex back is the woman who, above anything, makes herself a priority. She knows her emotional stability is more valuable than a man who makes her irrational, places self-doubt in her mind, or leaves her in a state of turmoil. She keeps the controls to her happiness planted firmly in her own hands.

Pleading does not get a man's attention, quietness does. If you have let Mr. Ex know you love him and want to make the relationship work once, you need not repeat yourself a second time. Doing so makes you sound like a broken record. He heard you the first time. To be the woman he pursues, ignite a feeling within him that tells him you are the one he's been looking for. If you lose his respect, he won't give you the time of day. How would you feel if a man begged you to have him in your life? You might take him back for a little while, but you would have lost the respect you once had for him. And once the respect is gone, that's it – Game over. Let the fat lady sing!

Men don't chase desperate, clingy women. When you act clingy and desperate, he'll think something is wrong with you. Having the date me, pick me, love me mentality isn't going to get a man's attention. In fact, it makes him run in the opposite direction.

Thirty Days of No Contact

Thirty Days is just one single month. You can handle anything for thirty days. By starting no contact now, you are jumpstarting the healing process. Understand the only actions you can control are your own. You are the only person who can control your emotions and make your exit without losing your mind, pride, dignity, and, most importantly, your self-respect.

Taking a step back for thirty days gives you time to look at things from a different perspective. It makes you stronger and wiser in ways that hopefully bring you new-found happiness. You may realize that you don't want Mr. Ex back at all.

Give the "Love" Hormone time to Wear -Off

You may have heard of Oxytocin, also known as the "love" or "cuddle" hormone. It's the "happy" hormone released into your system, sending signals to your brain telling you that you're in love with someone. The happy feeling you feel when you receive text messages and phone calls that make your heart skip a beat. *Oxytocin.* When you have an orgasm, oxytocin is released into your system and essentially tells your brain you are addicted to that man. Here's the kicker: There are reports that the hormone is also released when your relationship ends, or someone you love starts to pull away. To some degree, it's what makes you want to *do more and try harder* to persuade someone to love you. It's telling you to send the forty-eighth text, call one more time, or that it's perfectly fine to drive to his house at 3: 30a.m for closure.

Don't let it take over your emotions. Give it time to get out of your system. In thirty days, when you're thinking clearly, you may wonder why you ever gave Mr. Ex the time of day.

If you feel like you can't do this alone, find a "breakup bestie." A breakup bestie can be a friend, your mother, sister, aunt, or anyone who has a pulse that will hold you accountable for keeping your sanity and behavior in check. Who you pick should be solid as an oak. A person you can depend on in your greatest hour of need. One who will be there when the going gets tough. A breakup bestie is not one who will agree with anything you say or do anything you want them to do. You've probably heard, "A good friend will bail you out of jail, but your best friend will be sitting next to you saying, 'damn that was fun.'" For our purpose, you should find a good friend who will tell it like it is regardless if what they say hurts your feelings. He or she won't agree with you just to go with the flow. They will tell you how the cow ate the cabbage regardless if you want to hear what they say or not.

I want you to get at least one person on board for two simple reasons. One, you are far less likely to cheat and allow your crazy side to come to the surface if you have someone who will hold you accountable for your actions. The second is because life is always better with a trusted friend who will encourage you to bitch up and stand up for yourself.

Chapter 2
How to Recover If You've
Broken the No Contact Rule

∞ ∞ ∞

"There are no regrets in life, just lessons."

-Jennifer Aniston

*I*f you are reading this chapter to find out if you have broken the no contact rule, chances are you already did. Did you drunk dial after a few margaritas? Send forty-two text messages within an hour and a half? Stop by his office? Send an accidental text intended for someone else? Did you seek revenge? Steal his cell phone? Hack his email? Have ex-sex? Are you demanding an explanation for the breakup? There are hundreds of scenarios that, in the sober light of day, leave you feeling embarrassed, ashamed, humiliated, and in search of a way to regain an ounce of integrity.

It's easy to break the no contact rule when you are distraught. We all know we can't control our fingers when they're governed by our hearts. Calling Mr. Ex during the middle of the night to have your questions answered seems perfectly valid after a drink or two, right? Wanting answers to your questions seem perfectly logical.

You want to prove to Mr. Ex that you are a strong woman. You want to project an image of confidence. You want to come off as if you have everything under control. Instead, your willpower defied you and left you all alone to fend for yourself. If you made a mistake and behaved in a way you're not so proud of, the only thing left to do is forget you did it, forgive yourself, and move forward. So simple, yet so hard. It shows that you are human. It shows that you had a weak moment. It shows that you are vulnerable. The no contact rule is a suggestion to help you through a tough time. It isn't a law passed by Congress. You made a mistake. Don't beat yourself up because you revealed you are capable of being weak. Even the most exemplary women have fallen victim to allowing their emotions to override their good judgment. It only proves you loved him.

You are not the first woman to break the no contact rule and won't be the last. The next time you are in the same situation, you'll know how to handle disappointment and hurt in a mature, dignified way. Learn from past mistakes. When a man sees you handle your struggles in a decent, respectful way, it reveals you have an honorable character.

Reasons You May Be Breaking the No Contact Rule

➔ **The breakup blindsided you:** In boxing, they say it's the punch you don't see coming that knocks you out. In romantic relationships, it's not the expected that throws you for a loop. It's the unexpected. Mr. Ex was probably planning his exit for weeks in advance. He's had plenty of time to process his feelings, weigh the pros and cons, and make plans for his future. On the other hand, you didn't see it coming. You're broken hearted and still processing your emotions. You are upset because he made breaking up look so flipping simple. One day you were with the man you thought would be with you for the rest of your life, and the next day you feel as though you have experienced a death in the family. You want the person who you depended on to relieve your pain.

→ **You are still bonded to Mr. Ex Hormonally:** Remember the love hormone "oxytocin" we talked about in chapter one? It's taking over your emotions right now. It's telling you, "No man could ever replace Mr. Ex." The truth is any man who can make you reach an orgasm can make you feel the same way. Understand your heart is going through withdrawals. All it needs is time to recover.

→ **You are obsessing about what *was* instead focusing on moving forward.** When you obsess over anything, it means you're giving that one thing too much of your time. Too much of your energy. Too much attention. Too much thought. You must change the channel in your mind. When you start thinking about Mr. Ex, redirect your attention. Usually, in the middle of the night is when you want to reach out to him the most. Do something to refocus your attention. Turn on a movie. Read a book you find interesting. Reorganize your closet. Do anything but reach for that phone.

If you've slipped up, swallow your pride and admit you were wrong. With the right person, this makes a huge impression. Do you believe you owe him an apology? If so, do the honorable thing and apologize. When you say a simple, "I'm sorry," It proves you're the bigger person. It reveals you're secure with yourself. It shows the real you -- a mature woman who can admit she made a mistake.

Bitch Up!

Once you've said your peace, start over again with Day 1 of no contact. That's right... start over from the beginning. What do you do when you have been bucked off a horse? You dust yourself off and climb back in the saddle. When you're scared of flying, the only way to overcome your fear of flying is to board a plane and fly again. With round two of no contact, you absolutely must stick to your guns. A man may forgive you once, but if you continue to prove you are dysfunctional, chances are he won't be so forgiving the second time around. The good news is, no matter how bad you believe you messed up, the sun will still rise tomorrow. The earth will continue to rotate on its axis. As cliché as it sounds, life goes on, and so will you. Don't agonize over yesterday's regrets.

∞ ∞ ∞

"Falling out of love is like losing weight. It's a lot easier
putting it on than taking it off."

ARETHA FRANKLIN

The minute you make up your mind to start no contact, the little devil sitting on your shoulder will try to persuade you that sending one last little text won't hurt anything. In your mind, you'll find any reason to justify contact. Have you ever had a conversation with a friend, and suddenly, they tell you not to turn around and look at someone who just walked into the room? Your first reaction is to turn around and look. It's the same feeling with no contact. When you finally make up your mind to do it, your first impulse is to pick up the phone.

No magic formula will make no contact easy, but there are ways you can change to be successful. Start by refocusing your mind and redirecting your attention elsewhere. There are deviations from your normal routine you can and should alter to make it more bearable. You are readjusting, learning to live without Mr. Ex in your life. Change can't occur on its own. You have to break a few eggs to make an omelet. You must take baby steps to ensure your emotional happiness. Remember your end goal and plan backward. If you're trying to move on entirely or hoping he wakes up and sees what a mistake he made by breaking up with you, making simple changes will make your life so much easier.

Change His Ringtone

When you go from a daily routine where you receive phone calls and text messages on a regular basis to dead silence, it's hard. Painstakingly hard. The sudden inactivity from your smartphone of choice brings you heartache. You pray every minute you'll get a new message alert from Mr. Ex. Every single time your phone dings, you get your hopes up only for them to be crushed when you realize it's just a friend or your dear sweet mother randomly checking on you.

Right now, change his ringtone. One woman explained just by assigning Mr. Ex a unique ringtone, she was able to change the way she reacted to message alerts. If you genuinely feel you aren't strong enough to handle a text message from him, block his number for the time being, so that you will have no expectation or disappointment of not hearing from him. You can also set his contact to "do not disturb." You will receive the message but won't receive an alert. Do whatever you need to do to get through this time.

Change Your Screensaver

Who is your celebrity crush? Google his name and click on images. Pick out your favorite picture and save it to your smartphone, iPad, computer screen, or anything else you may have.

Let it be the first thing you see when you pick up your phone or turn on your computer. If you live in the dark ages and don't have anything to save it to, print it, buy a frame and place it on your nightstand, so it's the first thing you see in the morning and the last thing you see at night. A picture gives your mind a visual of someone (other than Mr. Ex) who you admire, adore, and think is handsome.

Clean House

Whether you want to get Mr. Ex back or are ready to move on to the next chapter in your life, it's essential to start with a clean slate. Right now, more than ever, it's time to do some house cleaning. Box up sentimental items that serve as reminders and cause you to get depressed. I'm not asking you to throw out pictures or burn them (unless you want to throw them out or burn them) instead neatly store photographs and other things dear to your heart in a box and place them on the top shelf of your closet, out of sight. I say "neatly" because I believe in treating your past with reverence.

Do you want to move on entirely? Then it's time to take one last walk down memory lane, say goodbye to the good times, or the bad times and then get rid of those items. This one little step helps heal and makes room for new love in your life.

While you're going through each room, cleaning out old memories and making room for new, gather any items that should be returned to Mr. Ex whether you believe this breakup to be permanent or temporary. Take the initiative to return his belongings as soon as possible. Don't wait to be asked, and don't assume he doesn't want his belongings returned.

What to Return

✓ Toothbrush
✓ Shaving cream
✓ Cologne
✓ Clothes/shoes
✓ Keys
✓ Garage door openers
✓ Cds. DVD's
✓ Anything he left behind
✓ Engagement Ring

If he hasn't left too much behind, a good option is to pack it neatly in a box and return by mail. No note or explanation required. When he opens the box, he'll recognize his stuff and know where it came from. There is no need to write a sappy closure letter.

If mailing is not an option, place what he left behind nicely in a few boxes. If you live within driving distance, drop them off at his front doorstep when you know he is not at home. The reason it's important that he not be home is that it's too soon to face him. His ego will tell him you're using it as an excuse to contact him. Your emotions are too fragile. By leaving boxes on his doorstep, or somewhere safe, it sends the message you are *not* trying to see him one last time.

One question I'm often asked is, "Should I contact him to make arrangements to pick up his stuff? My answer is there is just no need. Don't give Mr. Ex any reason to believe you are *trying* to keep the lines of communication open. If you can't mail or drop off at his home, find a mutual friend who can make the delivery on your behalf.

Another commonly asked question is about engagement rings. Engagement rings should be returned if the marriage didn't take place. It's the admirable thing to do, and in some states, it's the law. So, do what is honorable, take the high road and return an engagement ring before he has a chance to ask for it back.

What to Keep

✓ **Any gift he gave you.**

When it comes to gifts, I believe in a "no returns" policy. A man has no use for presents he gave you, and he should not expect them back. The no return policy goes both ways. If you gave a man a gift, don't expect or ask for it back regardless of the costs.

Gifts given to you while dating are yours to keep. Jewelry, clothes, art, perfume are all gifts. Gifts are given to someone with no expectation of payment or return. The only thing you are expected to do when given a gift is to say two simple words, "thank you." You are under no obligation to give them back. And why would you? What use will Mr. Ex have for a pair of earrings, a sexy piece of lingerie, or an oversized stuffed teddy bear?

Some women want to return every single gift they've ever received. Some use returning past presents as a reason to contact Mr. Ex. Some do it to seek the closure they need to move on. They want to erase memories. If keeping gifts is hindering your ability to move forward, get rid of them. One woman wanted to rid herself of the gifts she had received after a bad breakup. Instead of returning them, she gave the more expensive gifts to a charity, which auctioned them off to raise money for wounded soldiers. By doing this, she helped herself move forward and raised money for a worthy cause—a win-win.

Other women line the back of their closet shelves with a treasure trove of gifts they've collected from former flames over the years. If you take the time to gather gifts he's given, you can decide what you want to do with them later. Do you want to keep wearing the gifts he gave you? If wearing it makes you uncomfortable, store it in a safe place out of sight. Same with clothes. An important rule to remember is to have patience and think before you act in haste.

Friendly Reminders

→ **Don't Procrastinate:** Make any returns within two weeks of your last conversation. If you can do it within a week, even better. There is no need to drag this out longer than it must. Pack and deliver.

→ **Don't Write a Goodbye Letter:** The reason you should not enclose a handwritten note is to prevent him from having a strong read on your feelings. Resist every temptation urging you to write a letter explaining how you feel.

→ **Don't Trash his Personal Belongings:** Pack his things neatly in a box. Don't cram or toss them in a plastic trash bag. If he left clothes behind, wash, fold, and pack them before placing them in the box. Men are expecting the worst, so throw him off guard by taking the high road by showing respect to his personal belongings. The same principle applies when returning his things to his home or apartment. If he has a house, you may be tempted to throw the boxes in his front yard. Instead, remember to always strive to be the bigger person. Stack boxes neatly by his door with his name written on the front of the box.

→ **Return what is not yours:** If you have something in your possession that was not given to you as a gift, return it. Don't initiate a conversation or send a message asking for a list of items that need to be returned. Don't make it complicated. If you didn't receive it as a gift, the right thing to do is return it. If you didn't pay for the item out of your own pocket, return it. It's what an honorable woman would do. When you keep something that isn't yours, it's stealing.

Any woman can make a burn pile, strike a match, and watch Mr. Ex's stuff go up in flames. Any woman can gather clothes and throw them in the front yard to prove she's pissed. Any woman can take a pair of scissors and cut up clothes into tiny pieces. And maybe you are that woman. I'm not here to judge. It's possible Mr. Ex has done something so wrong that he deserves to have his shit strewn in his front yard. Another approach is to rise above and be better. If Mr. Ex has done something so horrible to make you want to destroy his belongings, is it really necessary to lower your standards to his level?

When to Ask for Your Stuff Back

By returning any items he left behind, hopefully, he will reciprocate by returning anything he has of yours. Before you send a message asking for something you left behind, decide if it's worth it. Can you live without it? Women have written to me about CDs, DVDs, their favorite pillow, and while I'm not making light of those items, they can easily be replaced. If he has a key to your place, I would go to the local Home Depot and buy a new lock before I asked for it back. My thought is if you can replace it easily, replace it. If it's not something you truly need or want, you may be using this opportunity as a clutch to hang on to Mr. Ex.

Give him time to return your things on his own before reaching out. Wait two weeks after the breakup before requesting them. If you must contact him, send him a quick text, straightforward and to the point with a plan to collect the items you left behind.

Chapter 4
Give Him Something to Miss

∞∞∞

"It's better for people to miss you than to have seen too much of you."

EDWARD NORTON

The main reason to stop reaching out to Mr. Ex is very simple: *To make him miss you.* A tried and true way to accomplish this happens to be the one thing that is the most difficult. It takes willpower, self-control, patience, and restraint. The one thing being *silence*. Silence hits a man where it hurts, his delicate ego. Women can't stand the thought of distancing themselves from the ones who just broke their hearts. You want for Mr. Ex to hear you and connect on an emotional level. The idea of going silent terrifies you because you feel you'll be forgotten. You believe by talking to Mr. Ex and sharing your feelings, you can convince him to change his mind. But in fact, silence is what it takes for a man to miss you. Remember, it's the empty can that makes the most noise.

It's no newsflash men don't like to talk about their feelings. With a few exceptions --They have no problem speaking up when they are hungry, horny or watching their favorite football player retire. They either have an erection or a snack in hand. Most men would rather go in for a prostate exam than discuss their feelings on a good day, much less right after a breakup. When he hears you say, "We need to talk," he'll look at you like you just killed his dog. So, let him off the hook for now and don't put him in a position to explain his actions. If you know you are annoying Mr. Ex -- stop.

It should go without saying he can't miss you if you're like an irritating fly trapped between a screen and a window, buzzing and banging around frantically. When a man tells you, he needs a break, open the door for him so he can hear the bells of freedom ring loud and clear. Make it clear the last thing you want to do is keep him from being happy. Let him fly as free as a bird. And then go silent, sit back, and wait for the dust to settle. He's waiting and anticipating for you to have a mental breakdown, act irrationally and cry hysterically. Over lunch with his friends, he'll brag about how hard you're taking the split. This behavior gives him the validation he needs to justify the decision to break up was the right one. He may even feel blameless because you were depriving him of his precious freedom and independence.

When you do the opposite of what he expects, after a couple of months, he'll be racking his brain, crying to his friends, "I can't believe she thought I was serious." The silence is what makes him feel abandoned. That's when you reverse the breakup. To give him a brush with death, do the opposite of what your natural instincts are telling you to do.

For example:

☞ **You want to express your feelings.** Instead, delete his contact information so you won't be tempted to reach out. Write your feelings down on paper. Put them in a safe place and read them at the end of each week. In a couple of weeks, as you reread the words you wrote, you'll begin to wonder what in the hell you were thinking.

☞ **You want to create an elaborate scheme to get his attention.** Instead, sit back, prop your feet up and stop working so hard for his attention. Give him space and let him try to figure you out for a change. By allowing him space, your emotions remain in check. By keeping your feelings under control, you retain your power. By maintaining your control, you appear a bit aloof at the same time.

☞ **You want to get dolled up and have a girl's night out at the bar you know he frequents.** Instead, drop off the radar like a stealth submarine. Leave Mr. Ex wondering where you are? What you're doing? Who you are spending time with? Will he ever see you again? When you can make him curious about what is going on in your life, it makes him miss you even more.

☞ **You want to update your social media sites with attention-grabbing status updates.** Instead, retain a touch of mystery by refraining from posting, tweeting, or snapping. Many women ask if they should delete Mr. Ex as friends or followers. My answer is *yes*, and the reason is simple. You can't be mysterious if you are updating your status every fifteen minutes. If you keep Mr. Ex as a Friend on social media, avoid "Liking" or leaving comments on his status updates so as not to appear you are cyberstalking. Make him believe your day is far too busy to stay on social media.

I receive messages asking how to get Mr. Ex back immediately, as in overnight. Women want an instant fix. Understand slow and steady wins the race. I know you want the pain to stop. I know the uncertainty is causing anxiety. The problem is you can't fix it right away, and attempts made to do so will ultimately backfire. He will view you as psycho and consider himself logical. Understand the relationship is at the very least broken right now. It can't be put back together by casting a love spell, creating drama, composing a miracle text, or a desperately seeking closure letter. Give him time to experience what life is like without you.

The feelings of anguish, heartbreak, and despair you feel right now are precisely the feelings he will eventually experience if you pull the lever in reverse and make him feel as though he is losing you for good. Before he broke up with you, he mentally prepared himself for what was to come, which is why he's handling the breakup like a champ. You didn't have the luxury of being prepared. Right now, you are going through withdrawals. You miss hearing his voice. You miss receiving his text messages. You miss seeing his handsome face. You miss the affection and love he gave you. You miss the sex. Understand he received the same text messages. He received the same affection. He received the love you gave to him. To make him feel the same loss of your love, just as he has made you experience, give him a dose of his own medicine. That's when he'll be calling you for a second chance.

Men handle breakups differently than women do. Women immediately become upset and react emotionally for the simple reason they are caught off guard. Men, on the other hand, don't kick it into high gear and truly appreciate what they have until it's gone. *Completely gone.* It's just like the old saying, "You don't miss the water until the well runs dry." If you don't have the willpower and strength to be silent, Mr. Ex will never gain a full understanding of what life is like without you. The only way to make him experience life without you is to cease all communication. And the sooner, the better. Live, eat, breathe, and sleep the no contact rule as if your life depended on it. He won't miss you instantly. He won't need you immediately. He won't come to his senses and call professing his love, admitting he was wrong. Only after his heart aches for you does this happen. After four to six weeks, the severity of your absence from his life begins to sink in. And this is when it hits him like a ton of bricks, he's made a huge mistake. When the reality sinks in that you may be gone for good, he'll call your mom, best friends, and co-workers crying like a baby trying to find out what you're doing.

Chapter 5
Strive to Be the Woman He Fell in Love With, Only Better

∞ ∞ ∞

"The whole point of being alive is to evolve into the complete person you were intended to be."

OPRAH WINFREY

Often, it's only when life deals you a low blow do you get the wakeup call you need to realize change is in order. There's an old saying, "Build a better mousetrap, and the world will beat a path to your door." Apply this concept to your life. Be a better woman, and a better man will find his way to you. What do you need to do to make your life a better one? How do you elevate yourself to a higher level? Have you become routine, stuck in a rut? I'm not suggesting changing who you are in any way to appease Mr. Ex. Instead, I'm suggesting you look at your current circumstances and ask what you can do to be the best woman able to handle the next relationship that comes your way.

At one point in time, he fell in love with you. What kind of woman would he describe you as when the two of you met? Take an honest look in the mirror and ask if there was something you could have done differently to change the outcome. Have you changed (for the worse) in any way? When I receive letters from women, they often say something along the lines of how they now realize they depended too much on Mr. Ex.

Men and women both need their own set of friends and hobbies independent of one another. Without a healthy amount of freedom, a man will soon feel smothered. Before he makes his planned escape, he'll say, "We're just at different phases in our lives." "I need space." Or "I need to find myself." The same is true if he feels like you've made him your science project. If you're guilty of inflicting your expectations on him instead of letting him think and act for himself, he'll believe you're trying to change him, which makes him feel emasculated and imprisoned.

A woman's top priority should be to have something going on in her life other than a man. It doesn't matter if you are viewed as an extraordinary woman or an ordinary woman. Do you have an interest that entertains you, challenges you, and keeps you occupied? One woman I know took up horseback riding and went on to help disabled children pursue their dreams to ride horses. Another woman started volunteering at her local food bank, and another began organizing a charity event to raise money for cancer. It doesn't matter if it's revamping abandoned furniture you find along the roadside if it is something you enjoy independently. A man begins to change his tune when he realizes your happiness is not dependent on his presence. Some women have been without a man for so long they go along to get along even if it means being disloyal to her feelings. She wants love so badly she overlooks the obvious. She'll do front flips to make sure he's happy even if all she's getting is his scraps.

A man is giving you scraps if...

- ☞ He texts weekly instead of daily;
- ☞ He avoids taking you out on a real date only to call after midnight to see you;
- ☞ He expects you to drive to meet him regularly;
- ☞ He is only available for sex; and
- ☞ He acts as if this level of commitment is the best he can offer.

Did any of the above resonate with you? If yes, you're failing his test and are undeniably a man-pleaser. You're accepting his bad behavior just as you would accept a bad weather day. Bitch up, sister! If you want to see a gleam of respect in his eyes, call him out on the carpet and put an end to his unacceptable behavior.

When you first met him, chances are you both were light-headed in love. You showed him your best qualities, which is what made you attractive in the beginning. Use this breakup as a life lesson to strive to be the woman he fell in love with again, only better.

Begin to act like a "rare treasure." (See Chapter Six) This is when a man begins to realize how much he loves you, how great you are, how proud he is you are his girlfriend. I can hear you say, "But Leslie, how can I act like a treasure when I don't feel like one?" My answer is to get in the habit of acting like a treasure, even if you don't feel like it on the inside. In certain situations, I'm a firm believer in the "Fake it till you make it" notion. Sometimes when you're not confident, you must imitate confidence. The same applies when you don't feel like a treasure, dig your heels in and act like one anyway.

You may believe you're too old to date, not pretty enough, not thin enough, not successful enough. If you believe there is nothing special about you, a man will believe the same thing. Women can quickly come up with a list of all the negatives about themselves but scratch their heads for hours when trying to come up with a list of reasons they're good enough. Shift your thoughts in a new direction. Every day say to yourself, "I'm beautiful enough to have any man I want." "I'm loyal, kind, funny, trustworthy, patient, honest, and I'm a great catch." "A man would be lucky to have me." Get in the habit of acting like a rare, valuable treasure even when you don't feel like one.

Chapter 6
Don't Compete and Don't Compare

∞ ∞ ∞

*"Always be a first-rate version of yourself
instead of a second-rate version of
somebody else."*

JUDY GARLAND

In the mid-1990s Ellen Fien and Sherrie Schneider wrote a popular book that became a New York Times best-seller, _The Rules, Time-Tested Secrets for Capturing the Heart of Mr. Right_. I was in my early twenties when I first read their book of secrets. It's one of my favorite books that give women a set of do's and don'ts for dating. One of the chapters is titled, "Be a Creature Unlike Any Other." They wrote, "Being a creature unlike any other is a state of mind. You don't have to be rich, beautiful, or exceptional." They went on to give advice and pointers on how to act on dates to stand out and be noticed by men.

I so badly wanted to be a creature unlike any other. The problem was I didn't know how to be one. At that time, I didn't feel unique or special. I didn't have the confidence to pull off the author's suggestions. I was a full-time college student. I had a full-time job and didn't have two nickels to rub together. I wasn't rich,

Bitch Up!

I didn't feel beautiful, and I didn't feel exceptional. The women I admired were older, more mature, polished, classy, sophisticated, and successful. While growing up and even now, one of my favorite actresses is Brooke Shields. I would watch her movies over and over again. At almost six-foot-tall, she's thin, beautiful, always looks put together, and comes off as a bit mysterious. I would wish with all my heart I could be tall just like her, look like her and act like her. Even though I have never met her personally, knew nothing about her other than the roles she portrayed in movies, in my mind, I believed she was the definition of a creature unlike any other.

Twenty years later, I've come to realize how easy it is for a young woman to feel inferior when there are so many smart, beautiful, talented, successful women who inspire and influence our lives. Insecurity has no discrimination. Insecurity doesn't discern if you were raised with a silver spoon in your mouth, the upper-middle-class, or in the trailer park of a one-horse town. I've come to understand there will always be women who outshine us. What makes you unique, what sets you apart, what makes you a creature unlike any other, is how good you feel in your own skin.

Women spend hours getting dolled up for a girl's night out. They put on their best dress, highest heels, and hit the hottest nightspot. They are happy as can be until they notice other women close by wearing cuter outfits, which make them appear more put together. They become disheartened when they feel like they don't measure up. If you're not secure with who you are in your own skin, without even realizing it, other women will bring the lack of confidence you have buried deep down inside to the surface.

I want you to be satisfied and happy where you are in life. You may say, "I shouldn't have to change for a man," and I agree. But never become complacent when it comes to improving. Never stop reinventing yourself. Strive to be like a fine wine that gets better with age. When you are so busy enhancing and elevating yourself, making plans for your future, assessing your strengths and weaknesses to see what areas you can improve on, or accomplish your goals to fulfill your dreams, that is what makes you a creature unlike any other.

When you compare your life to another woman's, you'll always find something she has that you don't. It could be in the looks department. Her hair is long, and yours is short. Her hair is blonde, and you're a brunette. Her makeup is impeccable, and you are lucky to get to work with mascara on your lashes. The same is true when comparing materialistically. I've seen women depressed because they didn't feel like they drove a nice enough car, live in a beautiful enough house, or the numbers in their bank account weren't high enough. It's only natural to want what you don't have.

Instead, adopt a mindset of future expectations. "I may not drive the car I want now, but I'm happy with what I have." In the meantime, keep your car clean and shiny. You may live in an apartment but want a house. Adopt the mindset, "I love my apartment. I'm going to do the best I can to decorate, keep it clean, and let it reflect my personality." One day you'll have the house of your dreams. If you're struggling financially, instead of worrying how you're going to survive paycheck to paycheck, ask, "How can I better myself financially?" What is your strategy to make your life a better one? If you think you're never going to meet Mr. Right change your mindset to, "I'm ready, willing, and able to love. Any man would be lucky to have me." If you stay focused on your goals, you won't have time to worry about what anyone else is doing. You'll be too busy making your light shine brighter.

Comparing yourself to another woman will only make you feel insecure. In the back of your mind, you'll feel the need to be in competition with her on an individual level. I know there are better authors than I am. Chances of my book winning a Pulitzer Prize are slim to none. But here's the thing, I'm not going to give up doing something I love. Instead, I'm going to strive to be the best author I can be. I know many women are more beautiful than I am. That doesn't mean I'm going to stop trying. Each morning I'm going to sit in front of the mirror with all the makeup I have at my fingertips and do the best I can to enhance what God gave me to work with.

It's not healthy to compare to other women who may be in a different phase of their lives. When you see a woman who is smarter, thinner, more beautiful, who shines in areas you don't, you'll start to feel inadequate when you don't measure up. When you compare yourself to another woman, you'll be in a never-ending competition that will ultimately make you feel not quite good enough. Instead of concentrating on what someone else has, and what you don't have, focus on what you do have and make the best of it and be thankful. Having a grateful attitude makes your light shine brighter. Don't get discouraged if you're not where you want to be yet, your time will come.

Chapter 7
Don't Obsess About Mr. Ex's
New Love Interest --

∞ ∞ ∞

"Looking good is the best revenge."
IVANA TRUMP

$\mathcal{S}$ocial media has made it easier than ever to spy on Mr. Ex's new love interest. Some women use antics that make spies with the CIA look like amateurs while investigating the opposition. The thing is that just because we *can* do something doesn't mean we should. You may argue that it's harmless, but it is *harmful* to your emotional sanity. What can I say, I'm a believer in the old theory, "ignorance is bliss."

If she has a face only a mother could love, you'll be tickled pink. If she's beautiful, it makes you feel envious and less than. If she flips burgers for a living, you feel superior. If she is a pediatrician and you flip burgers for a living, you'll feel like a failure. I could go on, but my point is for your own sanity, peace of mind, and for your emotional well-being, refrain from looking.

During a horse race, blinders are placed over the eyes of racehorses to prevent them from becoming distracted. The blinders block the vision of the horses, so they can't see what is to the right, left or behind. The jockey wants the horse's eyes focused on what is ahead, rather than what is to the side or behind them. They do this, so they won't look at the horse next to them and lose a step. The jockeys want the horse to do the best it can and ignore everything else.

The same principle can be applied when comparing with other women. Don't waste your precious time on anything that is preventing you from living your life to the fullest. If you're obsessing over another woman's life, that means you're not concentrating on yours. Put your 'blinders' on, so to speak. Jealousy doesn't look pretty on any woman. You don't have to be a size two to be amazing; you can be a size sixteen and still rock it. It's all about confidence and how you present yourself. You just can't go around comparing to other women. And why would you try? Each one of us is made to be exceptional in our own way. Each of us has been designed by our Creator precisely according to His plan. And He called us "Very good." He didn't just call the redheads, brunettes, blondes, the size two's, the smart, the talented, the wealthy, the successful, the black women, the white women, or the skinny women "very good." He called us all "very good." And that includes the tall women, short women, women with grey hair, pink hair, the larger women, the women who barely get by and the quirky women all "very good."

Through writing books, I've met some of the most beautiful women who, on a scale of 1 to 10, are easily a perfect 10. I've also met women who would be considered a 5 or 6. Often these are the women who bounce back the fastest. I can't help but believe it's related to their sense of self. Their inner strength is so evident, I can tell just by the way they present themselves how secure they are in their skin. On the other hand, the tens are usually the ones who take a break up the hardest. I receive messages month after month from some of the most beautiful women who are still trying to comprehend how a traumatizing breakup could happen to them.

Being beautiful alone doesn't give you immunity from heartbreak. Marilyn Monroe, one of the sexiest women of our time, had her share of pain dispensed by men. Her competition, Jaqueline Kennedy, could not keep the President's eyes focused on her even with all her beauty, intelligence and class. Jennifer Aniston had to contend with Angelina Jolie. Princess Diana, even with her stunning beauty, was left alone night after lonely night while her Prince was entertaining Camilla Parker-Bowles.

Beautiful women are left devastated all the time because their boyfriend or husband began dating quickly after their split. One of the first things they point out is deficiencies in the new woman. They may point out how unattractive she is, comment on her weight, or make a list of areas she lacks in. My response is to stop worrying about her. I know it is easier said than done, but don't focus on her because by doing so, you're dimming your own light. Chances are the new woman knows nothing about you. You're not even on her radar. While you are wasting your energy obsessing over her, she's not thinking of you at all.

A real test of maturity is not to be critical and jealous of other women. When you're jealous, you come off as bitter, vicious, cruel, and insecure. If you verbally attack her looks or her character, the first thing you do is ignite Mr. Ex's need to defend her. Just as women are born nurturers, men are born with an instinct to protect. If you put him on the defensive, you'll chase him right into the arms of another woman. No matter how hard it is -- bite your tongue and keep your thoughts to yourself. It's best to act indifferent and stay silent.

Bitch Up!

There is such a thing as a "non-compete" clause lawyers use while writing a contract. It's a clause that prohibits an employee from starting a similar business in competition against their employer. The clause is used on the premise that when they are fired, an employee might begin working for a competitor or start a business. By doing so, it would give the employer an unfair advantage by utilizing information about the former employer. Ladies, adopt a "non-compete" mentality when it comes to contending with other women. Make up your mind you will not demean or lower yourself by competing to prove your worth, prove you're good enough, or to prove your loyalty. I've heard it said, "Girls compete with each other, women empower each other." If Mr. Ex has begun to date another woman, understand he probably took the initiative and pursued her all by himself. She may not even know you exist. How he treated you is not her fault. So why hold her accountable for his actions? I know it may be tempting to vie for a man's attention, but a better approach is to step aside graciously and let the other woman have the job. Having a non-compete mentality unveils a woman who is entirely confident, secure, and content with herself. And this is when you earn a man's respect, and everyone around you takes notice.

Thomas Muster is a former number one tennis player from Australia. During his career, he won eight Master 1000 series titles along with a host of other titles. Obviously, a very competitive tennis player. He took an eleven-year break from the sport and then decided to make a comeback. When he got back on the tennis court, he was competing with men nearly half his age. When speaking about his return to the sport, he was quoted as saying, "My comeback was not about winning or losing; it was about the feeling of being able to compete at top level again." When you go through a divorce or breakup where there is another woman involved, it's easy to look at that woman and feel the need to compete. However, a better decision to make is that you're not going to compete at all, but rather strive to be at your top-level once again.

It takes a mature, level-headed woman to step aside and let another woman pass her by without becoming angry and bitter. If you can hold your head up high and say, "You know what?" "I'm not competing with another woman." "Instead, I'm taking myself out of this equation." "I know how special I am." "I know how unique I am." "I'm not going to waste one minute of my energy focused on trying to impress anyone." "I know there is someone out there who will be better for me." A man who truly loves you won't lose his focus when another woman enters the room. The best revenge is to let her keep him. If he did it to you, he would do it to her. What goes around, comes around. A real man can't be stolen. Bitch up and let him watch your ass walk out the door.

What you may not realize or appreciate now is that new woman might be there to allow someone who is a better fit for you to be in your life. It may be the universe telling you someone better than you could ever imagine is waiting for you right around the corner. Trust the universe is going to give you someone better than you had before. One day you will look at this breakup as only a moment in time. You won't remember the pain, the hurt, or the sadness. You'll see this breakup taught you something which brought you one step closer to happiness better than you could have ever hoped possible.

Having a no-compete mentality is when you enter a class all by yourself. When you have this type of outlook, peace, as you have never experienced, will fall on you like a warm blanket. That will be when a man will see your light shine brightly. Whether he comes back to you or not, he'll view you as the one who got away.

Chapter 8
Be the Best You

∞ ∞ ∞

*"In order to be irreplaceable, one must
always be different."*
COCO CHANEL

I n the process of abiding by all the rules of dating, following all the do's and don'ts, we forget to do the one thing that makes us most attractive. *Keeping it real.* We've been taught to *pretend* it doesn't bother us when a man gets out of line. P*retend* it didn't bother you when he let you down. We're told to pretend, so our weaknesses are hidden. We have been programmed to believe it's better to disguise our disappointment than to show our vulnerability. We think, as women, we are supposed to have all the answers. We believe we must be like men and show no emotion. You may believe a man will think less of you when you don't have all the answers when the reverse is true. When you keep it real instead of superficial, you reveal your vulnerable side.

Disguising yourself as a perfect woman will never work in the long run. You won't be able to keep up the performance 24/7. When you are woman enough to admit you have flaws, you allow a man to see past the facade and see you are a real woman who struggles in areas—that you don't have everything in life figured out. By revealing your weaknesses, it proves you are strong. This is when a man steps up to be your knight in shining armor.

Remove the self-imposed pressure to be perfect by stop living to impress, stop acting a way that isn't natural to you. Just stop pretending to be perfect. If a man doesn't love you enough to work through the hard times, in the beginning, I can assure you he won't love you through the hard times years from now. A man who truly loves you will accept you for the woman you are, inadequacies, shortcomings, quirks, and all. Some women handle the stresses of life better than others but make no mistake even the most put-together women are far from perfect.

There is just no such thing as a perfect woman, just as there is no such thing as a perfect man. We live in an image-obsessed society. We are told to dress a certain way. Act a certain way. Live a certain lifestyle. And if you do these things, you'll have a perfect life. Learn from the French women who have a 'no fuss' mentality. They don't come off as if they are trying too hard to impress anyone because guess what? They don't try at all. They don't strive or seek perfection.

If you must act a certain way, conceal your struggles, hide your fears, it keeps you from meeting the right man for the job. A man is looking for the real deal. A real, genuine, unique, down to earth woman. Not the fake you, not the pretend you, not the perfect you. He's looking for the woman he can love right now. What's important to portray is that you continuously strive to elevate your life for the better. Show you're doing the best with what you were given to work with. Admit that you're not everything you want to be but show you are determined to work toward your goals of being a better woman throughout your life. When you are doing your best to advance yourself, even when you're not there yet, it earns a man's respect. And that's when you become perfect in his eyes.

To be a catch lower your guard, stop pretending to be the perfect woman and start being the real, unique you. Some women work overtime to make their lives appear easy, and that's not a bad thing. It's just not for every woman. To be real, you must take off the disguise of perfection and understand by being vulnerable, you reveal the real you. Be comfortable with saying, "I don't have all the answers." When you can stop wearing the veil of perfection, that's when peace will wrap itself around you, and the perfect man for you will show up. It won't matter you're not where you want to be in life. It won't matter that you have three kids. It won't matter you don't have it figured out. A man can't be a Superhero if there is nothing to fix. If you did have everything under control, he would feel as if there was no room for improvement.

Take off the superficial disguise and get back to the real you. Your head may be jam-packed with doubts, flooded with insecurities. Perhaps you live a lonely life. Being the real, authentic you reflects your vulnerability. Come to terms with areas of your life that desperately need upgrading, tackle the problems head-on, and plan for change.

Maybe you're not where you think you should be in life. You may feel like you don't make enough money. You may feel you don't drive a nice enough car. You may feel you don't live in a good enough house. You may think you're not pretty enough. You're not skinny enough, or this enough or that enough. At some point, let go and say, "You know what?" "I'm enough." Flip the switch in your mind and start saying, "I'm pretty, I'm smart, I'm loyal, I'm honest, I'm trustworthy, I'm doing the best I can at this point in my life." Change the dialog in your mind, and while you're getting dressed, every morning, repeat to yourself, "I'm enough." "I'm a great catch." "A man would be damned lucky to have me."

If you can understand this principle, what one man doesn't view as valuable, another man will regard as a precious treasure. You may have several relationships in your adult life where a man just doesn't recognize what a treasure you are. They may not notice all the good you have to offer. They may not respect you, value you, or appreciate you. It's not that you are not a wonderful woman... you're just not the right, wonderful woman for this one, particular man.

When Mr. Right comes along, you won't have to play games. You won't have to try to manipulate him. You won't have to jump through hoops trying to win him over. Mr. Right is the man who will be there for you day or night, rain or shine. He'll be there for you without you having to ask. You won't feel as if you must prove to him why you are qualified to be his girlfriend. He will make you feel respected. He will make you feel bright and shiny. He'll make you feel loved, which only enhances your beauty. Mr. Right will love you for you, not the fictitious woman you're trying to be. He'll inspire you to be a better woman just as you will inspire him to be a better man. He'll love you for who you are, not what you do.

So why continue to waste your time on Mr. Ex, who may never be there for you? Why would you want to force someone to love you? Your time is far too precious to waste on men who don't appreciate what you bring to the table. If you can adopt a new mindset: *I'm only giving my time to a man who makes me feel appreciated, loved, and respected.* When you let go of the wrong man, you make room for Mr. Right. It's hard to realize when Mr. Wrong is, in fact, Mr. Wrong. Chances are he's a good guy. He may be good-looking and charming. Just because a man is *good* doesn't mean he'll be good for you. Be mature enough to recognize when he's just not good enough for you.

Each one of us is a work in progress. We can't do everything on our own. We can't be perfect, and men don't expect perfection. What they want is the real you, the Real McCoy. A man wants honesty. And when you can be honest and acknowledge you can't do everything on your own, you're showing the real you. Stop pretending as if you have all your ducks in a row. You don't have to try to portray an image of perfection. Life isn't hunky-dory every day. Start being real. Stop waiting for the perfect job, the perfect apartment, the perfect hair, the perfect body, the perfect wardrobe, to find the perfect man for you. A man is not waiting for the perfect cleaned up version of you. He wants an authentic woman who is comfortable being real, not only to him but herself also. And when you accept yourself the way you are, knowing you are doing the best you can every day, this is when you will experience absolute happiness, freedom, and peace in your life.

Chapter 9
Stop Giving It Away

∞ ∞ ∞

*"Give a man a free hand, and he'll run it all
over you."*

MAY WEST

hen is it okay to have sex after a breakup? Each circumstance is different, and it depends on factors only you can consider. For some women having ex-sex makes them feel less lonely. Others believe by having sex, their chances of getting him back increase. Chances are you care a great deal about Mr. Ex and would love nothing more than to express your love with a night of heated passion.

You may say, "Leslie, since we broke up, he's been texting me, telling me how much he misses me and how much he wants to see me. What do I do?" Just because he can type a message doesn't mean he loves you or wants you back. Until he is professing his love for you, making plans to see you in the sober light of day, stepping up his game to make the relationship work, stop giving up the goods. Even after a breakup, a man will show up for sex, just as one will show up for a homecooked meal. But why go through the hassle for someone who has made it clear they don't want to see you any longer. When it comes to sex, a woman wants to know why, and a man wants to know where? It's been said there are three ways to tell if a man is lying to you or not... before an election, during sex and after fishing.

It can take months for a man to realize how much he misses you, cares for you, and loves you. Until then, keep in the forefront of your mind that Mr. Ex told you he no longer wanted to be with you. This means he made the decision all on his own you're not the right woman for him. He wants to move forward, without you, to explore other options. *That means he hurt you.* Does it seem logical to want to have sex with a man who just broke your heart? I hope not. I hope your standards are higher than settling for just sex. And don't get me wrong, I'm all for just sex. I'm just not for just sex with someone who made a conscious decision to break up with me. Unfortunately, just sex doesn't guarantee the love you want.

What does get you closer to the really good, terrific sex? I'm talking about the really good stuff you may have never experienced because it comes along with a man who makes you feel loved, instead of feeling wounded. He makes you feel confident instead of insecure and doubtful. Mind-blowing sex doesn't come from the guy who tells you he loves you, yet makes you break into the ugly cry because his actions don't reflect his words. Talk is cheap. If a man's words lack meaning because his actions don't reflect the kind of love you expect, perhaps a better realization is you're not only settling for crumbs– you're being treated like crumbs. And what happens to crumbs when they fall on the floor? They get walked on. Take a little time to wait on Mr. Right.

Waiting for sex with Mr. Right has significant benefits. Not only does it comprise of mind-blowing lovemaking that leaves your heart pounding out of your chest, but it also includes having his arms wrapped around you while you sleep soundly throughout the night, breakfast the next morning and a kiss before he heads off to that job he wants to impress you with. Additional bonuses include phone calls the next day, dinner the next night, and flowers for no reason at all. This is the kind of love I want you to expect from now on.

Where women go wrong is by believing sex alone will get a man back. Just as sex didn't keep him by your side, in the beginning, it can't win him back in the end. Using sex to manipulate your way back into his life will ultimately fail. If you forego the work to make him feel the emptiness of life without you, he'll still have sex with you, but you'll be the one broken-hearted when he leaves after having the big O. Which only proves his penis may be committed to you, but his heart isn't.

If you believe there is a chance of a reunion, your best option is to hold off until he sincerely wants you back with all his heart. And this can take months. Just as making a man wait at the beginning for sex is advantageous to you, so is making him wait for it after a breakup, if you want him back for keeps. Why? Because forbidden fruit is always the sweetest. Remember to think of your long-term goals and have a plan in place. You want him to miss you so much he comes to his senses and realizes he can't live without you for one more minute. So, putting off sex for a little longer is a small sacrifice to make to get what you want in the long run.

It could be the love hormone oxytocin is actively telling your brain that you are still in love. You may try to justify in your mind all the reasons it's a good idea to have sex after he just dumped you. It's familiar territory. You know what he likes, he knows what you want. There are no first-time jitters. The downside is if you believe that by having sex, you will soon get back together. It could break your heart all over again if things don't work out the way you hope. How are you going to feel if he leaves without spending the night? What if he doesn't call the next day or the next?

Bitch Up!

Give your heart time to catch up with the actual events that are taking place. Keep a level head by understanding just because a man wants to sleep with you doesn't mean he loves you or is contemplating a future with you. He could just be cleaning out his pipes. To prevent short term pleasures from being long term regrets, wait for his actions (not his words) to prove his love for you.

Chapter 10
Does Making a Man Jealous Work?

∞ ∞ ∞

*"To keep your character intact, you cannot
stoop to filthy acts. It makes it easier to
stoop the next time."*
KATHARINE HEPBURN

At some point the idea of enticing a man back to your side by making him just a little bit envious may enter your mind. Wanting to make a man green-eyed with envy is only natural. Even if you don't like to play games, wanting to catch his attention and make him jump in his car to chase you down may be your dream come true. However, tread ever so lightly if taking this route. Understand making a man jealous on purpose can backfire. Just as revenge is a dish best served cold, so is attempting to make Mr. Ex jealous. The end goal is not to make him jealous in a callous, heartless way, but to ignite his gut instincts to step up and be the man you need him to be.

The no contact rule is a perfect way to create just the right touch of suspicion without going to drastic measures. When a man doesn't know what you are doing for an extended period, it begins to make him uncomfortable. He slowly begins to sense the connection the both of you once shared is now in jeopardy. Fear gradually takes over his mind with thoughts you have found someone to take his place. Letting his imagination run wild is usually enough to do the trick. When he starts to imagine another man pleasing you sexually in ways that he believed only he could, he'll swim against the tide to win you back.

Just as you have over analyzed each detail, by using the no contact rule correctly, eventually, a man's mind will go into overdrive overthinking the unknown. To make his imagination run rampant, change your profile picture to one of you, living it up having a superb time. You don't have to be dressed up like a runway model. You don't need to post a picture with a mystery man to make him jealous. You only need to plant a small seed in his mind that you are enjoying your life to the fullest. And maybe you're not enjoying life right now, but that's information he doesn't need to know.

Mark Twain once said, "You can't depend on your eyes when your imagination is out of focus." Sitting back, allowing his imagination to take over is much more potent than intentionally, blatantly making him jealous. There is no need to tell Mr. Ex you have a date next week, or even let him know there is another man interested. A man only needs a touch of suspicion to enter his mind to imagine the possibility of a new man moving in on "his territory." That's what makes him want what he can't have. Suddenly, he'll act like a guard dog ready to protect you, his prized possession, from any threats. A touch of suspicion alone usually motivates a man to step-up, if he genuinely cares for you, because now he feels slightly defenseless.

Written by Leslie Braswell
Use Social Media to Your Advantage

When women ask, "How can I possibly get my ex back when we've stopped communicating?" and "How will he know what I'm doing when I've started using the no contact rule?" When celebrities go through breakups, the tabloids report what parties they're attending and with whom they're spotted out having dinner with. The average woman doesn't have TMZ readily available to capture her every move. What a woman does have at her pretty little fingertips are the many platforms of social media. Using social media alone won't win a man back, but women should use it to their advantage. Even though I strongly urge you not to cyber stalk Mr. Ex, the truth is it's a hard temptation to resist. Even if you have unfriended or unfollowed him, chances are both of you share mutual friends you're comfortable enough with to ask to view the others page to see what's new in their lives. And just as you check his social media accounts, I can assure you he does the same to yours.

Do

- Post pictures that make you look amazing.
- Post pictures of you and your girlfriends having an incredible time.
- Post pictures while vacationing.
- Post pictures of family and friends, which reflect your fantastic life.

Don't

- Post sad selfies that make you look like a hot mess.
- Post sad status updates about the breakup.
- Post old pictures of the two of you with a caption professing your undying love.

Bitch Up!

- 🌸 Update your status with sad music.
- 🌸 Update your status with rants about men.
- 🌸 Immediately post a picture with a "new" boyfriend.
- 🌸 If you have unfriended him, don't send another Friend request.

After a man has delivered the devastating breakup news, he has a vision of you sitting on the sofa, surrounded by crumpled tissues, crying into a pillow, with mascara running down both cheeks. By doing the opposite of what he expects throws the planets out of alignment for his ego-minded brain. I know you may not feel like putting on a brave face when your heart is breaking. But put on a brave face, you must. And make-up. A touch of makeup never made any woman look bad. The show must go on, and you must portray yourself as a survivor and adopt a survivor mentality. Sometimes all you need is a Kodak moment to throw him off guard to make him change his tune. Use great photos to your advantage.

To use the no contact rule while using social media, first, go silent for a couple of weeks to prove you are not using it in a way to make him jealous. To be subtle, incrementally show him and the world you are moving on, having a great time with friends, doing great at work, or anything else which casts a favorable light on your life. This is when Mr. Ex stops and says, "I wish I were there with her" or, "Wow, she looks great." Just by proving a breakup doesn't break you but instead makes you stronger makes you more appealing. It's what will make him check your profile fifteen times a day in hopes of catching a glimpse into your life. Why? Because when a man sees a wall, the first thing he wants to know is what's on the other side.

Chapter 11
How to Work with Mr. Ex

∞ ∞ ∞

"If you don't like the road you're walking,
start paving another one." –
DOLLY PARTON

S ince, most people, spend more time at work than anywhere else, it's only normal to fall for a co-worker or even a supervisor. It can be challenging to keep your head held high while also suffering from a broken heart. One of the questions I'm asked is how to handle the no contact rule when you see Mr. Ex five days a week? Ideally, you would have an understanding beforehand that regardless of what happens in the future, you both would agree to keep time spent in the office professional. Granted, we don't always do what is ideal and chances are you didn't seek advice on office romances before it started. The good news is if your end goal is to get him back, you have an advantage over women who do not have the chance to see their ex on a daily basis.

Here are a few helpful tips to help you through your workday. If you are genuinely suffering from a broken heart, feel as though you can't function without crying or are just unable to focus on your job, use your sick or vacation days to take some time off work. But frankly, I don't recommend hiding. It's time to show your grit by showing up the next day looking like you just stepped out of a salon.

The end goal should be to keep the work atmosphere from becoming awkward for you, Mr. Ex, and all your co-workers. Before polishing up your resume to go job hunting try to keep your sanity and reputation intact by first, pulling it together.

→ **Fall in love with your job:** Take all the energy you have, and dive into work with a newly revived confidence. Do you remember how enthusiastic you felt on your first day? I bet you thought it was the best job ever and how blessed you were to have this new incredible opportunity. Adopt a new mindset to love your work and reawaken the feeling you once had when you first began.

→ **Keep it professional:** Let your professionalism shine by treating Mr. Ex precisely the way you would handle any other co-worker. Live by the four Ps. Polite, professional, productive, and proficient.

→ **Avoid Mr. Ex.:** If you work in different departments, divisions, or buildings, this will be easy as you probably don't have daily contact. If you know where he parks each morning, park your car on the opposite side of the parking lot. If he arrives at 8:30 a.m. every day, make a point to arrive fifteen minutes before him. Be in your office or sitting at your desk by the time he walks in. Do the same for lunch and when leaving for the day. If you have a meeting together, arrive on time, and leave promptly at the close of the session. Don't linger, don't try to speak to him and avoid making eye contact. Act as if you barely noticed he was in the meeting.

→ **Communicating:** When you do work together on a one on one bases, keep it professional and to the point. If possible, send an email instead of communicating directly in person or by phone. When you initiate an email or call him directly, stick strictly to business, be direct, and avoid rambling. Refrain from allowing your personal feelings to take over and profess how much you miss him, love him, and can't live without him by your side.

→ **Keep it classy:** Avoid talking about the breakup with fellow co-workers. There is no reason to spill the details about your love life with people who are merely innocent bystanders. Speaking poorly about Mr. Ex does nothing but lessen your character and make you appear bitter, immature, petty, and small. Criticizing Mr. Ex will do nothing to diminish his reputation but will damage yours to the point of no repair. Keep it classy by taking the high road. When co-workers ask about what happened, respond by saying with a sweet smile, "It just didn't work out." Enough said.

→ **Tying up Loose ends:** Avoid returning Mr. Ex's personal belongings to him at the office. Exchanges should take place on your own personal time, not the companies.

→ **Look amazing:** One thing you must always remember is men are visual creatures. Don't show up to the office, looking like an unmade bed. Show up each day as if you are going to meet the Queen of England. Don't wear your heart on your sleeve. Just because you are broken-hearted doesn't mean the entire world knows it. When you take time each day and put forth effort in your appearance before you go to work, it makes you feel better, impresses others, and makes you more productive. Look so good he scratches his head and contemplates why he ever let you slip away. Bitch up, put on some lipstick, and focus on being the kind of employee you would want to hire if you were the boss.

→ **Send flowers to yourself:** One of my favorite stories came from a woman named Dedra. She had been involved with a man at her office for over eight months when he broke up with her. One day she emailed me and was so depressed because Valentine's Day was approaching. She felt kind of sad because she knew she would not be receiving flowers at the office. So many of her female co-workers were married, and she knew they would receive flowers from their husbands. She told me she was absolutely dreading going to the office on that day and was considering calling in sick. I gave her this advice: Go to a flower shop and order two dozen red roses and have them delivered on Valentine's day.

She did take my advice; only she took it a step further. She went to three different flower shops and had a flower arrangement from each delivered to her office. By the end of the day, she was the most popular woman at work. Both men and women were stopping by her desk, complimenting her flowers. When she was asked, "Who's the lucky guy?" She simply responded, "I don't kiss and tell." As for Mr. Ex, his head spun at a 360-degree angle. He couldn't keep his eyes off her the entire day. He called her within the week.

Create Distance and Detachment

When ending a relationship with a co-worker or boss, the two most crucial factors is to keep it classy and drama free. To make Mr. Ex miss you, even though you see him five days a week, create distance and detachment. It may not be possible for you to cut off all forms of communication. But you can control how you act and portray yourself. Go over and beyond to be friendly to everyone *but him*. To him, act *indifferent*. This alone should get his testosterone level to rise.

Put distance between the two of you by avoiding him like the plague. Don't make excuses to see or communicate with him. Make him feel as though you would rather have a root canal than reach out and talk to him. You accomplish this by keeping communication direct, to the point, and professional. Have a problem that you would typically ask him for help? Before seeking his assistance, try to be a problem solver and figure out another way.

When you are in his presence, he must sense you have disconnected from him emotionally. Don't laugh at his jokes. Don't look at him with sad puppy dog eyes. Convey with your actions, body language, and attitude, you view him as nothing more than a co-worker. This move alone will usually make him step back in your direction. During this time, show the entire office what a great catch you are by rising above, holding your head high, and depicting yourself as a woman with class and dignity.

Chapter 12
How to Handle the No Contact Rule When You Have Children Together

∞ ∞ ∞

"It doesn't pay to get discouraged. Keeping busy and making optimism a way of life can restore your faith in yourself."

LUCILLE BALL

To function each day with a broken heart is tough. Even tougher when you must put on a brave face while still having to juggle the responsibilities of being a single mom. Having a little one who depends on you to be there for them twenty-four hours a day, seven days a week, can take its toll on the strongest of women. All you want to do is lie in bed in the dark, yet you have a little one who expects (and deserves) you to make breakfast every morning, get them dressed, off to school, help with homework, keep the house organized, attend after-school activities along with one-hundred million other things.

Written by Leslie Braswell
Don't Let a Child See You Cry

One woman confided to me she got through the first few weeks after her husband left by knowing that if she would just get up each morning and get her kids off to school, she could go back home and climb in bed until it was time to pick them up eight hours later. Each day before she picked her kids up, she would get out of bed, get dressed, and pull herself together so they wouldn't see her at her worst. To her credit, she managed for weeks without her kids knowing she could barely function. Each day she would just go through the motions to get by. She was crushed when her husband unexpectedly filed for divorce. She needed to be alone during the day to grieve, to be sad and cry.

It was obvious she loved her kids, but emotionally she was struggling. She was miserable, depressed, and even though she wasn't exerting herself, she had very little energy. I asked her what her main priority was. Without missing a beat, she replied her kids had always been her focus. I told her to start making dates with her kids. Be honest with them and tell them relationships don't always work out. But regardless if she was dating, married, or single, they would still be her main priority, the ones she loves the most.

Keep busy with your kids instead of obsessing over Mr. Ex. Play all the games they like to play. Watch a movie, read a book, take a bike ride, or go on a trip. Show them what a strong, independent woman looks like. Life is good with a partner when you have children, but it can be just as fulfilling if you don't. You can devote more time to your kids. You won't have to divide your time. You can focus your attention directly on them always.

If you are serious about finding someone to share the rest of your life with, from this day forward be selective with who you choose to invite into your life. Don't allow just anyone to have access to your heart or your kids.

One single mom told me that after fourteen years of dating men who she knew had no potential, she finally got serious about finding a quality man. She had dated players, bad boys, even an alcoholic. She dated these men on the side with no intention of introducing any of them to her children because she knew they were not "good enough." She started what she called the "three-date rule." She explained that she would agree to give a man at least three dates. If by the third date she wasn't convinced introducing her children was a good idea, she would move on to the next, without wasting her time. Within a year, she married a man who not only treats her like a queen but who is an amazing stepdad to her children.

Don't Be a Bitch Unless You Must

When you have one or more children with Mr. Ex, the no contact rule can't be strictly followed. Always exercise good judgment and common sense. If you have younger children, who can't communicate directly on their own, interact with Mr. Ex in a calm, cool, collected way. While you can't go entirely without contact or communication, you can control what you talk about.

- ☞ Don't use the child by creating ways to contact Mr. Ex.
- ☞ Don't avoid contact altogether. If Mr. Ex sends a text wanting to know how the little one did at school, be polite and answer.
- ☞ Don't be a bitch unless you must. If Mr. Ex wishes to swap weekends and it doesn't interfere with your plans, let him. If he says he is going to be two hours late dropping off

little Jimmy and it doesn't inconvenience you, don't cause a fuss.
- ☞ Don't speak poorly about Mr. Ex. Kids love their parents, even the bad ones.

Try to be accommodating as much as possible without being a doormat. If Mr. Ex wants to do something that is a conflict for you, in a calm, mature way, explain why it's not possible.

The goal is to reflect you are moving on with your life. Be pleasant when you communicate by phone or text. Avoid discussions about getting back together until he brings it up. When you must see him face to face, make a point to look your best, not as if you just rolled out of bed. Some think if they look sad and depressed, it wins his sympathy when, in fact, it does the opposite. No man will race back to a "Debbie Downer." If your goal is to get him back by making him feel as though your happiness and life depend on him, you'll lose. Playing the role of "poor pitiful me" never works.

Instead, when he comes over to pick up the kids, open the door with a smile on your face. Be happy and accommodating when you have to deal with him. This immediately makes his radar go off, wondering what's new in your life. Keep conversations limited to your little one and keep your personal feelings at bay. Don't inquire about his personal life, and if he asks about yours, be vague. The goal you want to accomplish is to keep from coming off as desperate or needy.

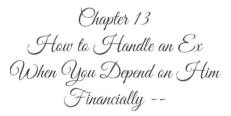

Chapter 13
How to Handle an Ex
When You Depend on Him
Financially --

∞ ∞ ∞

"Courage is being scared to death...and
saddling up anyway." --

JOHN WAYNE

*O*ften, I hear from women who don't know how to handle a breakup because they are financially dependent on a man. Starting over from scratch scares the hell out of them. They are too scared to leave because doing so would alter their financial stability. They believe they won't ever be able to recover money-wise from a split. This is especially true for women whose husbands or exes have always handled paying the bills, made financial decisions, or made more money. For the first time, they're setting up a new household, paying their own bills, mortgage, and preparing a budget to manage their finances. Chances are the income they live on is much less than they were accustomed to before the split.

It's never easy responding to an email asking, "What do I do if my boyfriend broke up with me, and I have no money to move out of our apartment." First, get over the panic. You do this by mentally preparing and planning for changes that are to come. The first place to look is to your family. Will they be able to help with the monetary costs of moving? I know the thought of running back to your parent's house isn't the ideal situation. However, four walls around you and a roof above you should be your first priority. For now, forget about the extras you're accustomed to and focus only on the essentials you need.

If you are living with Mr. Ex even though he has broken up and asked you to leave, start finding small ways to put money aside. Is moving in with family or friends an option? If not, tell him you are saving for a place of your own and will leave as soon as you can. Do your research to find out how much it will cost to move. In the meantime, is there a second bedroom you could use? If not--claim the sofa. Create a bit of distance to let him know you are giving him space.

Get Back to Basics

If you have plenty of cash or can depend on family to help you establish a new residence, the better off you will be. If, on the other hand, you are like many women who struggle, your first priority should be to cover the essentials. The essentials being a roof over your head, a bed to sleep in, a car to go back and forth to work, money to keep food in the fridge, and the lights on. When you know the essentials are taken care of, breathing will become a bit easier, and worry a little bit less.

Now may not be the time to buy a new car. You may have to settle for a used one. You may have to settle for a 'staycation' instead of the expensive vacations you are accustomed to taking. You may not be able to afford shopping sprees you once were accustomed to, but little by little, bit by bit, you can add small extras to your life.

One friend of mine loved laying out by her pool every summer. Her idea of relaxation and therapy was floating in the water and soaking up the sun. After she divorced, she purchased a home without a pool. When summertime came around, she bought a thirty-dollar wading pool large enough for a float for one. She didn't let the fact she didn't have a luxury pool in her backyard get her down. Instead, she chose to get back to the basics, and when she did, she was just as happy.

Dealing with emotional turmoil coupled with new financial burdens can be mind-numbing. Facing so much change all at once leaves some women in a state of shock. Breaking up when financially dependent on another can make you feel hopeless, scared, and alone. It means a change of lifestyle, but isn't that always the case when a romantic relationship ends? Remaining calm and at peace is a hard feat to accomplish when living with the weight of the world on your shoulders. What is important is not to make a bad situation worse by making life-changing decisions in haste.

Make a strategy that places your life back on track. Maybe you haven't worked in years. If so, be proactive and start looking for a job. Perhaps you need to look for an apartment or a new house. Act now to ensure your basics are covered. Get excited about making a new, better life for you.

Self-assurance comes when you have a full understanding of what you are dealing with and have a plan in place to accomplish your goals. Instead of looking at this change as a disappointment, view it as a new opportunity for improvement. Perhaps it means that you must find a job. Finding a new job means you have a chance to meet new people and learn something new. Most importantly, when you start planning for your future, you gain self-confidence because you have a clear understanding of what must be done and a plan in place. You begin to believe in yourself because you know what you need to do to move forward for a better future. A plan makes your life operate more efficiently. And when you begin to implement small changes, changes for the better start to happen unexpectedly. That's when you can breathe a sigh of relief.

Chapter 14
What to Do When You Are Stuck in Relationship Limbo -

∞ ∞ ∞

"A wise woman wishes to be no one's enemy; a wise woman refuses to be anyone's victim." –

MAYA ANGELOU

The term "limbo" is used to describe a state in which you do not know where you are going, what you are doing, or where you fit in. You can be dating, engaged, married, or even stuck in limbo after a breakup. After a split, some women put their life on hold, waiting to see how things play out. If you've been on again and off again, you may not know if you are a couple moving forward, or if you are in a relationship at all. You are stuck in a rut. You know what you want but feel powerless to get it. Being stuck in relationship limbo is pure hell for the simple reason of the uncertainty of not knowing if you are single or not. Being creatures of habit, the uncertainty of living in a state of limbo drives us a little bit crazy.

You May Be in Limbo If...

- ✓ You don't know if you are officially his girlfriend. He hasn't asked you to be exclusive. He doesn't make plans or call regularly.
- ✓ He doesn't introduce you to friends, co-workers, or family.
- ✓ You are engaged, but your fiancé won't commit to a firm date, so you can book a venue, have invitations printed, and begin to make wedding plans. Regardless of how hard you try to get him to commit to a date, he won't budge.
- ✓ You have moved in with a man, sold your home, let your lease go, and he's stalling to seal the deal with a ring and a ceremony.
- ✓ Your boyfriend broke up, but you're still going back and forth, on-again, off-again trying to make it work.
- ✓ You have his child but no ring.
- ✓ He's told you, "I don't know what I want."

There are several reasons why you should come to terms with the fact you may be living in relationship limbo. The main reason to put an end to living in limbo hell is it isn't a happy place to stay. When limbo enters your life, it brings along insecurity, unhappiness, loneliness, and depression. By nature, women like to nest and have clarity as to where they belong. We want to have plans in place. Not knowing where you stand is like walking on glass. You know if you step too hard, you're going to break it. So, you walk around with an uneasy feeling, afraid to make waves.

The first step is to acknowledge you are, in fact, living in limbo. Often in the early stages of dating, after only a few dates, some women don't even know if they are classified as "the girlfriend." And some women have been dating for two, four, or seven years, and the guy will not budge to buy her a little ring and move on to the next phase.

Bitch Up!

It's time to bitch up!

Before you proceed, mentally prepare for the worst, which will turn out to be the best thing for you in the long run. There are only two ways it can go, and you shouldn't be afraid either way he chooses. Regardless if you like it or not, this will give you the one thing you need the most, *clarity.* He'll either shape up or ship out. The worst that could happen is he makes his exit. I can tell you if he chooses to walk out, you'll be sad, heartbroken, angry, and miserable. And then, shortly after, acceptance will follow along with peace and happiness. I know you don't want him to leave but mentally prepare for it so you can keep it together. Prepare for the worst, expect the best.

The other alternative is you get his attention and start having the relationship you want. *One that is moving forward toward marriage.* Either way, after this phase, you will no longer be stuck in relationship hell.

It may take a week or longer to have the right frame of mind. If you feel as though you have nagged, pushed, pressured, and given ultimatum after ultimatum until you are blue in the face, stop. Don't say another word or drop another hint. Don't mention the words relationship, marriage, or the other four-letter word men find so frightening --*more.* Don't bring up the future or ask, "Where is this headed?" Start being the fun, confident, and carefree woman he became attracted to in the beginning.

Delayed or deferred gratification is to resist a smaller but more immediate reward to receive a more substantial, more enduring reward later. In your case, you want to move the relationship to the next level, and you want clarity, stability, and peace of mind. Remain calm, cool, and collected, always. Up until this point, your guy has been calling the shots and steering the ship. The end goal is to have you back behind the steering wheel, navigating your life in the direction you want it to go. The only person who has kept you trapped in limbo is you. He keeps you dangling like a puppet on a string because you won't bitch up and cut the ropes. No matter how many times you warn him, you won't get his attention until you stop talking about life *with* him and start living life without him. He won't really believe you'll go until you dare to walk away, moving onward.

If you are the one who initiates contact by calling, texting, or suggesting get-togethers because he doesn't, stop immediately and slowly ease back. Remember that securing plans for dates is his job. Don't take away his responsibilities. Whether you realize it or not, you are doing the courting, chasing and pursuing. It's time you reverse the roles. You might say, "But Leslie, if I don't call him, he won't call me." Wish him farewell, sister! Kick him to the curb! You will never be happy in a relationship if he's not capable of dialing your number to hear your voice. The most comfortable, confident women don't have a single doubt in their minds about the love their significant other has for them.

You might also ask, "How am I supposed to have a conversation with someone who never calls to make a real date?" The answer is if he doesn't call to make a real date, there won't be a conversation. There is no need for conversation. His actions have conveyed all the information you need to know, which is you are not in a relationship. Consider yourself officially out of *limbo*-land. This is your big red warning sign to discard him like a tissue. For the rest of you who have invested *years* of your time, energy, blood, sweat, and tears, it's time to have the conversation that will move you to the next phase of your life.

The Conversation

Bitch Up!

Have the conversation at a restaurant where you have his full undivided attention. Look as fabulous as you possibly can. You should be mentally prepared for it to go either way. If he doesn't tell you what you want to hear, there should be no tears, crying, sobbing begging, cursing, pleading, or persuading involved whatsoever. The one principle real women who know their worth understand is being desperate and clingy are cheap commodities.

When dinner is almost over in a calm, sweet way, remind him it's been a year (or however long), and you feel as though the relationship isn't moving forward. In a non-threatening way, gently explain you do *want* to be married and would like to begin to make plans to move forward. Tell him you completely understand if marriage is not what he wants but ask that he be respectful of the fact it is important to you. If marriage is *not* for him, it's only fair he tells you now. And then sit back in complete silence. The less you say, the better. Wait for him to speak first.

Hopefully, he will agree, want the same life you want, and the two of you can move on to dessert. If, on the other hand, he tells you, "I don't see marriage in my future," or, "Now is not the right time for me," be prepared to say, "I understand how you feel, and I respect your decision. I hope you understand I want to be with a man who shares the same dreams and values I do." And then be prepared to pick up your purse and walk away. No tears. No convincing. No begging. No pressure. Leave with a smile on your face and a spring in your step, knowing men are just like parking places... a good one always becomes available sooner or later.

What you've done in a dignified way is to tell him you have standards for the way you want to live your life. When a man knows he must step up or step aside, he'll either make plans for a change, or he won't. It's really no more complicated than that. Either way, you won't waste more of your precious time waiting for something that would never come to pass anyway. After this conversation, regardless of what he chooses, it's time to get back to your life. It's time to focus on you. You should now have the clarity you need to move forward. You know you aren't content floating around in relationship limbo, so is there a reason to stay? Is there a reason to continue to do something you know doesn't make you happy?

There is a reason that living in limbo should be unacceptable to you. For starters, you deserve an incredible, fantastic life. Your cup should runneth over with love. When you're stuck and don't know where you're going, it's all too easy to put your amazing, incredible life on hold, hoping, praying, and waiting with bated breath for a man to come through and live up to your expectations.

An excellent question to ask is why you are afraid of ending a relationship that is not making you happy, content, or fulfilled? Why are you loyal to a man whose actions don't bring you peace and clarity? Chances are the man you are waiting for isn't waiting for you. He's not putting his life on hold. While your waiting, guessing and wondering what he's up to, he's out in the real world living his life, happy as a clam. He's having his cake and eating it with a silver spoon.

While remaining in limbo, you won't give other men a fair chance because you are pinning all your hopes and dreams on a man who is making you a little crazy. Mr. Right could be waiting right around the corner, but you won't bump into him because you're sitting at home on a Saturday night waiting for someone who is letting you down. If you have a backbone at all, bitch up and make him do a little guessing of his own.

You may believe you want your life to be a certain way, and that you can't be happy unless you have this particular man. Let go of the power he has on you. Let go of the control you are trying to have on the outcome of your life and allow the universe to step in and guide you. Take your rose-colored glasses off to see things for what they really are. Start by being brutally honest with yourself and, more importantly, live in reality. The reality is life is not meant to be spent floating around in limbo, bouncing from nowhere to nowhere.

When you make it known, the earth still rotates on its axis, even when he is not in your life, that's when you'll wake up his snoozing ego. Odds are he has adapted comfortably to treating your life like a revolving door, coming and going. Take the first step by slowly pulling back, one step at a time. Instead of answering every text within twenty seconds, don't respond. Do the same when he calls, let it go directly to voicemail. Wait until he calls back a second time, and without being brash, abrupt or bitchy, simply state, you have plans. Have excuses ready, and on the tip of your tongue, so you're not racking your brain trying to come up with one at the last minute. Here are some examples of ways in which you can be busy the next time he calls.

→   You're going shopping with friends.
→   You're having dinner with friends.
→   You are volunteering at the local humane society, walking homeless dogs.
→   You're too busy tonight, but next week you're available.
→   You bought tickets to see your favorite band/Broadway Play/movie.
→   You are washing your hair.

Give any excuse you can that leaves him with the feeling you are not sitting around on pins and needles waiting for his call. If he hasn't called in three weeks, give him the impression you barely noticed the time-lapse.

Written by Leslie Braswell

Often women who are stuck in limbo don't realize a breakup as a divine intervention getting you ready for a better relationship. Each time you go through a breakup, it teaches you something and moves you closer and closer to the relationship you were destined to have. You may be hanging in there because being with *Mr. Maybe* gives you comfort, a certain amount of security. You may have a mindset that having somebody is better than having nobody. And that outlook may work for a while but understand "settling" never lasts. Women thrive on stability. If you are in a relationship for years and you still don't know where it's going, recognize you are limiting your ability to be happy. Continuing to depend on a man who has proven to you he's going to keep you right where you are isn't going to move you forward. When you remove him from your life, even if it's painful, even if you don't like it, you are opening your mind and heart for a better replacement.

There is a whole world out there waiting for you to live it. There are new friends to meet, old friends to catch up with, new movies to see, white sandy beaches to sink your toes into, a family who loves you and sunsets to watch. There is a man out there who will love you for you. A man who will never place a single doubt in your mind. Be patient... he will come when you least expect it. In the meantime, stop putting your life on hold for someone who isn't making you their number one priority. Don't let another day go by saturated with worry, drama, anxiety, fear, and uncertainty. You know you're moving on when you accept the split. That's when peace will engulf you. You've done everything you can do, it's out of your hands, and you can accept it for what it is. Don't wait one more minute for someone to make you happy. Make yourself happy.

Chapter 15
When to Walk Away

∞ ∞ ∞

"A smart girl leaves before she is left."
MARILYN MONROE

*H*ave you wondered if you are wasting your time, questioning where you fit in the picture? If you've asked this question, there is a problem. Relationships take two people who are willing to put forth their time, effort, and energy to make it work. Often, one person is in denial and doesn't want to face the reality of the situation. You know you need to bitch up and walk away if:

○ **You don't know when you will see him again.** When a man respects you, loves you, and wants to be with you, he will move mountains to see you and often. It won't matter if he's a busy brain surgeon. He'll make scheduling time to be with you a top priority.

○ **You are the director of the communications department.** If you are the one dialing his digits, the first to always send a text message, the one who must plan to see him it means one thing: you're the pursuer, the hunter, the chaser. You're doing a man's work for him. A man who is crazy about you won't need prompting or a friendly reminder you're still out in the world.

○ **The only contact you have with him is via text message.** Real relationships consist of actual face to face, man to woman conversations. If the two of you haven't looked at each other in the eyes for some time, the reality is you don't have a relationship. He could be multitasking and have several women on his Ferris wheel of love.

○ **He doesn't make time for you on weekends.** You've cleared your schedule and have been waiting all week for a call making plans for the weekend, and nothing ever pans out. When the weekend comes around, you're left alone because he didn't make time for you. Now you're all dressed up with no place to go.

○ **He doesn't reciprocate the same kind of love.** Your intuition will tell you when you feel like you love him, more than he loves you.

○ **He doesn't take you out in public.** When he does make plans, it's at the last minute. If he always orders takeout, and the two of you eat in, that should be a sign. A man who is proud of you will want to show you off.

○ **He Forgets Your Special Day.** He forgot your birthday. Men who are seriously dating want to make the woman they are with happy, happy, happy. If he isn't putting forth the effort to make you happy, happy, happy, then you are not significant to him.

○ **He doesn't spend holidays with you.** On holidays like Christmas, New Year's Eve, and Valentine's Day, he's missing-in-action. *Dump him.*

○ **He hasn't given you a title.** A man who hasn't given you a label such as "girlfriend" after a significant amount of time is keeping his options open.

○ **He only calls when he wants sex.** If the only time you feel loved, treasured, or special is in between the sheets, then you

82

are nothing more than a booty call, friends with benefits, or whatever you want to call it. He's using you as a midnight call girl, and you are letting him. *Stop giving it up!*

Just like friendships, there comes a time when relationships should be assessed, and the importance of said relationship should be reconsidered. If you answered yes more times than not, don't let the sunset tonight without dumping him. You can't do the tango with just one person...it takes two. If you are the only one taking little love steps to keep it going, then it's classified as a one-sided relationship. If that small inner voice, I call a hint from God, is telling you that you love him more than he loves you, trust the hint from God. Don't be the woman who waits around like a puppy.

Dating a great guy who's wrapped around your little finger will never keep you up in the air as to when you're going to see him next. If he treats you to lunch, he wants to know if you're free for dinner. While having dinner on a weeknight, he's making plans for the weekend. If he's not making plans to see you, he will offer an explanation without you nagging him to explain as to why he's not taking you out. You'll never wonder if your brand-new iPhone is experiencing a glitch because you haven't received a phone call or text message within days. If he wants to see you as badly as you want to see him, he won't act like a predator who only comes out at night hunting his prey. He will want to take you out in the daylight hours to show you off because he loves you and wants everybody to know it. He will always make you feel better about being the woman you are, even when you don't feel good about yourself. He will answer phone calls and responds timely to text messages. When the going gets tough, you won't be wondering where he's at since he'll be standing right by your side. He'll be there for you when you face your worst days and there to celebrate your best ones. You'll never feel as though your heart and soul are being destroyed because of his poor choices since he always has your best interests at heart.

And guess what? He not only gives you all his love but *wants* to receive your love in return.

True Love Doesn't Hurt

I don't know who said, "Love Hurts," but I can tell you without a doubt, true, real love doesn't hurt at all. Love doesn't make one cry or leave one feeling insecure or full of doubt. Understand suffering while in a relationship is voluntary. What you allow is what will continue. And while it may be painful to accept the fact the person you want to love doesn't reciprocate in the same way you want, the hurt you are feeling is from that realization, not the feeling of love. To put an end to the pain and sadness someone is causing you, bitch up, trust your gut instincts, reclaim your power, and stand up for yourself by saying, "This isn't good enough." "I won't settle for the pain, uncertainty, and fear you're bringing into my life." Hanging on to hope that a man will change for the better may be wishful thinking. It may make you feel better, but understand it's preventing you from having the kind of love you deserve.

At a man's core, he wants more than anything to make you happy. Everything a man does is to amaze you, impress you, woo you, and show you, he has what it takes to keep you happy, fulfilled, interested, and by his side. Just as you love him, he will want you to feel that same love and will do his best every day to make you feel the same way.

You may have stayed in a relationship for months, even years, because you thought a man loved you. One question to ask is how he makes you feel, day in and day out? You must be able to recognize when someone loves you without question, without condition, whether you're having a good hair day or a bad one. Because living

84

with the uncertainty of whether a man loves you and has your best interests at heart, robs you of the very thing that provides you peace of mind. *Confidence.* You may wonder throughout the day if he's thinking of you. If he doesn't call, you begin to worry. When he's away, you're not confident he's doing what he says. You fear you're not doing something right or not doing enough. When your intuition is telling you something is right, learn to trust it, embrace it, and go with it. When your intuition is telling you something is wrong, learn to trust it also. The problem we all face is by ignoring our little inner voice alerting us something is not quite right because it isn't what we want to hear. And when we ignore our intuition, it bites us in the ass every time.

The absence of feeling loved makes some women kick it into high gear, working harder to please. Remember the love hormone oxytocin we talked about in Chapter One? Right now, it's telling your brain to do more and work harder. No matter how well you are performing, no matter how much you've done, you feel the need to do better and do more. You're not getting the love you need, so you make a grand gesture to *make* him feel loved. You're not getting the love you need, so you cook his favorite dinner. You're not getting the love you need, so you amp up the sex. Where you begin to lose your pride and dignity is when you start to operate under the assumption you need to do more, be better, and amp it up in between the sheets to win his love. And when it doesn't work out, you doubt yourself, feel insecure, and beat yourself up wondering what more you could have done to make him love you.

When living with the insecurity the unknown provides, you go through each day with a degree of doubt and anxiety. Negative thoughts invade your mind. You begin to think of the hard times you've had and get down on yourself. It robs you of your energy. You obsess over every aspect of your relationship. The doubt and insecurity may cause you to be depressed, which doesn't help you to be a better woman. As a matter-of-fact, it causes you to struggle more.

From this day on, adopt this new mindset: *Do less, expect more.* Expect a man to be good to you. Expect him to make you a priority. Expect him to do little things to make you happy. Expect him to be there for you on sunny days and during the storms. The mistake so many women make is by doing more but expect less. But here's the thing, a man worth a grain of salt doesn't want an insecure woman who doesn't view herself with high regard. He wants a woman who knows she is the best.

A woman who knows her value won't live with uncertainty for long. If you believe a man is stalling, turn around and walk away, give him the chance to follow you. He will either follow or walk away. And isn't that the clarity you need? When a man loves you, there will be no persuasion required on your part. You won't feel as though you must have it all together. You won't feel as though you must portray perfection. No, he will love the real, authentic you, shortcomings, struggles, hardships, and all.

When you *know* a man wants you, loves you, and will do anything for you, it gives you the confidence of an eagle, unafraid of storms. What separates the eagle from other birds is they are not afraid of storms. While other birds hide in fear, the eagle uses the storm to be lifted high above the clouds. No matter how bad the weather is, they continue to fly higher and higher. Just like the eagle, there will be times when you must keep flying even when it's storming. There will be times, even in a good relationship, where there are storms. There will be times where he won't be happy with you. There will be times when you won't be happy with him. But at the end of the day, you will still know he loves you without a doubt. You recognize he won't give up on you because nothing you do could make him love you less.

Bitch Up!

If a man loves you, he won't care if you look your best or your worst. He won't care if your struggling. He won't care if you're not at a place in life where you want to be. Instead, he will be the first to offer to help get to where you want. He won't need to express his love every minute of the day, convincing you because his actions prove it. He'll go over and beyond, treating you like a treasure. When he takes you to dinner, spends his time, his energy, doing the little things that mean a lot, he's making a point to let you know he loves you.

If you believe your circumstances give you a disadvantage, understand a man who loves you sees you in a different light. The little inner voice that whispers, "I know if I act a certain way, dress a certain way, have longer hair, a perfect hourglass figure, drive a nicer car, have a better job, then I'd know for certain he'd love me so much more." The problem with this type of love is that it is conditional. When a man makes his love contingent on you meeting specific criteria and living a certain way, that's limited love. Not real, authentic love. Don't try to perform to increase your chances. Just take the pressure off and be the authentic, genuine woman you are.

With your new adopted mindset, even if someone walks out of your life, know he just wasn't the right man for you. There is someone better on the way. Until Mr. Right shows up, bitch up, and stop settling for less. When you find you are working hard to *attain* his approval, when you feel as if you're working hard to *earn* his love, you'll know next time to take a step back and not settle for a man who leaves you in a state of confusion. Step aside and let him figure out his issues. Don't make your peace of mind dependent on whether a man is providing love to you. Love yourself.

Written by Leslie Braswell

If you dare to expect more out of relationships, guess what? You get more! Bitch up, stand up straight and tall and let the weight of all the uncertainty fall off your back. Redirect your attention to winning the end game and stop settling for less.

Chapter 16
Don't Live Bitter, Live Better

∞ ∞ ∞

"When you are happy, you can forgive a great deal."

PRINCESS DIANA

*J*ust as you can push people away with bitterness, you'll draw them to you when you are bright and happy. And I know there are times we all have bad days, but understand a great attitude along with a super personality goes a long way. It reveals you have let go of the past.

After your heart has been shattered, it's easy to let hurt consume your everyday life. You are disappointed, wounded, maybe even a little traumatized. When you are living this way, every waking moment tends to make your thoughts gravitate toward how betrayed you were. Perhaps you were cheated on, taken advantage of, or Mr. Ex disappeared without a trace. Maybe you just can't comprehend why he broke up in the first place. After all, everything was going great until the day it wasn't.

Every single one of us, at some point in our lives, have had bad things happen. Being hurt doesn't discriminate against different classes of women. You can be the most beautiful, successful, put-together woman, and still have gone through a traumatizing split. What distinguishes happy women from bitter women is one simple principle: Happy women have learned to forgive.

One woman explained how devastated she was after she found out her husband had an affair. She described her relationship as "perfect" and was completely blindsided when she discovered he had been having an affair on an ongoing basis. Articulately, she expressed how heartbroken she was. She just wanted to crawl into bed and sleep. She had a hard time focusing on work. She was so depressed she sought help through counseling. None of this surprised me. In fact, I thought what she was going through was normal. That was until she mentioned it had been *eight* years ago. My jaw dropped.

How could it be that this woman had held on to so much pain for eight years? Mr. Ex not only hurt her the first time, but she allowed him to continue to hurt her for eight more years by holding on to so much emotional baggage. I'm sorry, ladies...that's not acceptable. You just can't hold on to anger for so long. It's mentally unhealthy. You can't let the short time you have here on earth be consumed by reliving one wrong over and over.

When hurt, take time to mourn the loss. Do whatever must be done to comfort yourself during this time. If it makes you feel better to lay in bed in a dark room for a week, do it. If binge eating Rocky Road ice cream brings you comfort, eat it. If tequila with a dash of lime makes you feel better, bottoms up! If you want to cry and bitch to your friends about what a sorry S.O.B. he is, do it. And then find your inner bitch, throw back the covers, get out of bed and get on with it.

If you can look at it from a different perspective, and that is, every breakup you endure will move you closer and closer to the man you are destined to be with. This may be your first hard breakup. Do you realize you *might* go through four more terrible breakups before the man who sees' you as the woman of his dreams finds you? Every bad lunch date, dinner date, failed relationship, is preparing you to meet Mr. Right. Sometimes you have to date a few duds before you find a keeper.

Accept a breakup for what it is: The universe shaking things up to make room for a better man to enter your life. Don't wallow around in self-pity. Don't go through weeks, months, years of depression. It may be Mr. Ex's fault for the split. Maybe he was unfaithful... he's to blame. But if you're six months or a year down the road and still blaming him for hurting you, betraying you, making you unhappy, wake up and realize your happiness is your responsibility. Shame on you for not moving on faster. You just can't move on to a happy, content life if you're living in the past.

Bury the hurt, resentment, and bitterness to a place where your mind refuses to go. Whether it happened last night or eight years ago, it's called the past because it has no place in the present or the future. You can't move on to a happy place if you're obsessing about a relationship that didn't work out the way you wanted. Every day put one foot in front of the other to move on to a better life.

It's easy to say, "But he hurt me, he left me, he broke my heart into a million pieces." "That's why I'm bitter." "He doesn't deserve my forgiveness." Let me say that I am truly sorry this happened to you. If I could take the heartbreak away, I would. But I can't. I can tell you if you remain stuck in the past, if you continue to relive it day in and day out, you will let Mr. Ex continue to hurt you. He may not deserve your forgiveness, but I'm not suggesting you forgive him to make him happy, forgive him for you. Don't give anyone that much power over your happiness.

Written by Leslie Braswell

Alexander Graham Bell once said, "When one door closes another door opens, but we so often look so long and regretfully upon the closed door that we do not see the ones which open for us." If you continue to focus on the closed door, it will keep you from opening your heart to a new, better love waiting for you. Each breakup you go through is preparing you to be a stronger, more confident woman, for a better relationship. If you continue to live in pain, you won't be open to a new opportunity for love.

Don't let one lousy relationship ruin your chance for future happiness. You may have trust issues. You may feel the need to go around believing because one man hurt you, you will never be able to trust again. You may be angry or resentful.

To rise above and be better, deal with those issues so your heart and mind will be open to giving Mr. Right a chance. You must be able to trust the next man who enters your life. And to trust, let the anger, bitterness, and resentment go. Remember the old saying, "You can't let one bad apple spoil the bunch." Live by this rule: Trust until given a reason not to trust.

View change as a new opportunity. Each day there are chances for new beginnings. Crying over what happened yesterday, last month, last year or ten years ago won't bring you closer to a happy life. If you continue to obsess over what happened in the past, that's where you'll stay. Living with regrets of what could have been, what should have been, doesn't do anything to advance you to a better place. Living bitter, angry, upset over what Mr. Ex did to you, will hold you hostage.

When someone does you wrong, understand it doesn't define you as a woman. Let worry, disappointment, mistakes, bitterness, betrayal, and hurt roll off you like water on a ducks back. A woman who possesses an ounce of self-worth is mature enough to understand it's not her fault. She doesn't carry someone else's baggage on her back. Instead, she digs her heels in deep and makes her mind up she'll be a better woman. She knows a better, greater love is still in store. She understands she is not defined by what someone else did to her but by how she handles the hard times.

How to Let Go

Often, I'm asked, "How am I supposed to move on?" "How do I let the hurt go?" The first step is to quit giving it a platform by stop talking about it. When you stop talking about it, you'll eventually stop thinking about it. Make a vow to yourself that you won't bring it up to your best friend, dear old mom, or that sweet lady in the check-out line. Not a peep.

How do you stop thinking about it? Start redirecting your attention. Is there a reason to relive the hurt every single day? When you allow hurt, disappointment, and heartbreak to set up residence in your heart, that's what you will portray to the world. One of the main reasons you can't move on is because you're talking about it, and if you're talking about it, you're thinking about it.

One sure-fire way to run a new love interest off is by coming off bitter and angry. One man told me about the night he took a woman out on a date. Her divorce had been final for over ten months, but the way she talked about the ordeal was like it had been yesterday. He said the entire night she talked about how her husband had cheated. The unkind things he did were relived in detail the whole evening. He knew she wasn't over the breakup because all the anger, hurt, and bitterness was transparent. He never called her again.

Written by Leslie Braswell

As nicely as I possibly can, I'm telling you this: Nobody cares. Your best friend may care. Your mother probably cares. People you barely know...do not care. When you're tempted to bring up Mr. Ex, just stop. If you forget and accidentally find you are talking about him, laugh it off, and immediately change the subject. Talking about a man who cheated on you, who did you wrong, makes you look bitter, and nobody wants to be around a scorned woman. It will eventually push everyone away. Later, after you've had several dates and he's fallen in love with the beautiful, kind, smart, funny woman you are, you can mention Mr. Ex was unfaithful. Keep it light and classy, and he'll think, "Wow!" "What a dumbass!"

The difference between 'bitter women' and 'better women.' is this simple principle: *Forgiveness.* Bitter women have not forgiven, and better women have. Forgiving Mr. Ex for whatever he did to you, whether he has apologized or not, will allow you to recover and move forward at lightning speed. Disappointment is a part of life. What I believe to be true for women to move forward without allowing disappointment to define them, is their willingness and capability to forgive. You are not the first woman who has been hurt and won't be the last. What separates a bitter woman from a better woman is the bitter woman will put on a fake smile while allowing the bitterness to kill her on the inside. A better woman smiles on the inside and out because within, she lives with a high level of peace.

Don't allow bitterness to consume you. Don't allow a breakup to cause you to be acrimonious. Don't allow it to take up permanent residence in your heart. You may be heartbroken now, but a new level of happiness is in your future. Don't let a breakup control your life. It's not going to ruin you. It's going to make you better.

Chapter 17

Love Yourself First

∞ ∞ ∞

"True love doesn't come to you. It has to be
inside you."

JULIA ROBERTS

hen, a woman, is genuinely heartbroken, the last thought on her mind is starting over. Going through the stages of grief, anger, denial, and depression is normal. It may be hard to get up, get dressed, and put on a brave face for your friends. Force yourself to do it anyway. The sooner you can get out and about, the better off you will be. I know it's hard. The message I want to relay is the pain, unbearable as it is now, is only temporary. Once you come to the realization it is not the end of the world, your heart will slowly heal, and you will go on to have a better life, one better than you could have ever hoped for or imagined, you'll have a new perspective.

You may believe you will never find love again because Mr. Ex was the best thing since sliced bread, and nothing can change your mind. Granted, if you were truly in love, the last thing on your mind would be to go out and date. You may think there will never be a man who can replace Mr. Ex. You may think no man will be able to measure up. The heart wants what the heart wants.

The problem with this mentality is if you believe it for too long, you'll adopt the mindset finding love again will be impossible. You've planted that seed in your mind, and the negative thoughts you believe to be true, become your reality. It becomes ingrained in your mind. If you continue to think you'll never find love again, you set that negative mindset into your everyday life. You won't be openminded to meeting someone new.

After a death, employers give their employees three days of bereavement to grieve the loss of their loved one. (Do I agree with this? Not at all. But if a mother who loses her child is expected to go back to work after only three days, I think you can pull it together after only a breakup.) Give yourself three days tops for not leaving the house. During these three days, go without makeup, stay in bed, cry as much as you want to cry and eat as much chocolate as you want to eat. Then get up, get dressed, and get out of your house. You must continue to do your part.

In the book, _Make Your Bed: Little Things That Can Change Your Life...and Maybe the World_, United States Navy Admiral William H. McRaven wrote, "You need an anchor point for your day, and sometimes that anchor is as simple as making your bed." "It will give you a small sense of pride, and it will encourage you to do another task and another." The same principle can be applied to us as women. Get up each morning and get dressed. When you look good, you feel good. Don't get me wrong. There is nothing more I enjoy than a day in my pajamas (other than a day in my pajamas without makeup). But I can't do it seven days a week. When going to work, running errands or meeting friends, put forth the effort to look good, if not for yourself, do it for others. For most women, it takes less than twenty minutes to put their makeup on each morning. And if you don't wear makeup, at least make sure your hair is fixed. Once you do it, you are done for the day. It makes you feel pretty, self-assured, and a little bit sassy.

Bitch Up!

Take a lesson from Alicia Keys, who decided to ditch the makeup and go all-natural. She performed on television, at the Democratic National Convention, and on The Voice without makeup. If she had shown up in a pair of yoga pants, hair like a cavewoman and no makeup, the powers that be would have had her committed. Instead, she pulled it off because, even without makeup, she still had pride in her appearance. She took the time to fix her hair, and her attire was impeccable.

If you continue to crawl into bed day after day, feeling sorry for yourself, all you're doing is nursing your broken heart. You're doing nothing to seek closure and move forward.

Adopt a new mindset of positivity and strength. To be inspired to find love, each day be open to the possibility of allowing love into your life. You must get out, every day, and invite love in with open arms. A man isn't going to knock on the door to your house or apartment and ask you on a date. A man isn't going to notice you while you're lying on the sofa watching reruns of Will & Grace. Muster up as much strength as you can to put one foot in front of the other to put yourself in a position to find love. Go out with your friends, visit your family and go places. What if Mr. Right is frequenting your favorite coffee shop right now? What if he is at the park walking his golden retriever this very minute?

When you do go out with friends, avoid talking about Mr. Ex. If he cheated on you, try not to relive the pain night after night. When you talk about it, you're feeding it. Remember, you are trying to move forward, not relive the past. When you obsess about what went wrong, you'll continue to live in the past. If you continue to think you will never find love again. If you dwell on those thoughts, you'll continue to live your life in that way. What you tell yourself each day is exactly the way you will live.

The same is true if you're down on yourself. If you say you're too old, too fat, too this or too that, you'll walk around life feeling too old, too fat, too this or too that. You will start to believe you are wasting your time. You may give up. Day after day, your inner voice has to say, "I'm beautiful, I'm smart, I'm funny, I'm honorable, and I'm a great catch." Push negative thoughts telling you, you're not good enough completely out of your mind. When negativity enters your mind, recognize it, and then repeat, "I'm beautiful, I'm smart, I'm funny, I'm honorable, "I'm a great catch." Repeat it over and over again, day after day, until it's ingrained in your mind.

I receive messages from women who are in a state of shock. Their minds are numb from pain. They feel as if their chance at love and happiness has been lost for good. They are so discouraged because they believe life isn't going to get better for them. The mistake we make so often is assuming a situation is permanent. The most important principle I want you to know is heartbreak is temporary. You will laugh again. You will live again. You will love again.

All women want to feel appreciated, cared for, loved, and special. When a man makes you feel that way, you'll walk with a spring in your step, your eyes will light up, and you feel good on the inside. We all want to have someone in our lives who we know, without a doubt, loves us. A good man who loves you, who builds you up, who tells you every day how beautiful you are is about as good as they come. My husband tells me every day he loves me, or how beautiful I am. And even though I don't need to hear it, I never tire of it. There isn't a man or woman alive who doesn't shine brighter when they are given compliments or gratitude is showed.

Expect More, Get More

Bitch Up!

There are many benefits of being in love and having a partner who gives you all the perks of being in a relationship. Expect to have a man who believes in you. Expect a man who is on your side for better or for worse. Expect a man to encourage you and bring out all your best qualities.

Where people go wrong is by becoming reliant on receiving the happiness, the love, the adulation from *someone* rather than providing it to themselves. What happens when that one source stops giving it to you? The loss of affection... The loss of love... The overall general loss of a man's presence in your life.

Mr. Ex made you feel special, loved, and appreciated. You've lost someone who made you happy. But if your happiness, self-worth, and entire world revolve around one person who suddenly decides to exit your life, then you're left dealing with a host of emotions. You may be depressed. You may get discouraged. You may not feel like you're good enough. You may ask, "What's wrong with me?"

Bitch up, my dear! The message I want you to take away is that your happiness, self-respect, and value as a woman should never be contingent upon whether a man is in your life or not. Yes, I know it's nice to hear sweet nothings. It's nice to receive roses that remind you someone in the world is thinking of you. It's nice to have someone take you to dinner. The problem is if your happiness buttons are only pushed when a man is feeding you compliments, expressing his love, taking you places, or sending you roses, then you will ultimately be let down. If the only time you're happy is when you're receiving the love someone else is giving you, that means you're not giving yourself the love you need. Who you date is not what gives you your value and self-worth. What someone does or doesn't do is not what gives you your worth. If your happiness fluctuates based on whether a man is in your life or not, you can count on the fact that you'll be disappointed and let down at some point. Don't let a man's love and admiration be the only proof you have that you are a treasure. Love yourself.

Even in the best relationships, men get busy. You can't be with a man day and night, twenty-four hours a day, seven days a week, for months, even years, and expect his priority to be your happiness every day. How are you going to cope when he gets too busy or preoccupied with work and can't be there for you? Most men have a full-time job, friends, and family of their own, bills to pay, hobbies they enjoy, and their own set of responsibilities. The last thing you want to be viewed as is another job. A burden on his already full plate. Don't misunderstand, a man who loves you will, above all else, want to make you a priority. Where you lose him is when he feels you are a second job, he'll get burned out quickly. Understand your value, self-worth, and happiness comes from within, not from an outside source. When a man is too busy to make your happiness his priority, you will remain at peace and won't become disappointed. When he's too busy with work to make time for you or is absorbed in a Monday night football game for three hours, he'll be happy as a clam that you're just fine on your own.

Once you begin to feel special, loved, and happy on your own, you'll stop seeking validation from Mr. Ex, or Mr. Right. You won't feel the need to kick it into high gear, working over-time trying to win approval because your emotional stability isn't subject to how you are being treated. When you adopt the mindset, "No endorsement needed," your relationships become better. You will be viewed as a treasure. The next time a relationship gets rocky, you will be mentally prepared.

In every hardship, endeavor to be a woman of substance. Don't let your emotional security, happiness, and sanity depend on how someone else treats you. Understand a breakup doesn't lower ones' value. How you handle it does. Are you mature? Are you watching what you say? Are you keeping it classy? Any woman can lose her bearings, lash out, curse, slam doors, and show her ass. But when a woman with substance goes through hard times, she gets through it not by losing her poise but rising above to come through stronger, by digging deep within and showing how resilient she really is.

Don't let a breakup or divorce make you feel as though you're not good enough, pretty enough, smart enough, this enough or that enough. You're enough! A relationship doesn't determine your worth. Possessing self-worth doesn't require you have a man by your side or someone else's last name. A woman of worth pays no attention to who is by her side or whether she's attained the approval of others. It means nothing to her because it just isn't required to make her feel good on the inside. Whether a man is in your life or not, walk with your shoulders back, head held high knowing within you are enough.

When a man is not giving you the reassurance, the compliments, the flowers, the proposal, then that's OK. You can reassure yourself. You can tell yourself how beautiful you look. You can buy yourself flowers. You can even treat yourself to dinner. You don't need his stamp of approval because you approve of yourself. Your happiness is not dependent on what he does for you, rather what you do for yourself.

Even in the best relationships, there will be a time when you have a disagreement. The disagreement can last a few hours, a few days, or even weeks. When this happens, you won't be told how beautiful you are; your praise won't be sung, and you won't feel appreciated. You'll be on your own, even if you live under the same roof. If you can't handle yourself in a dignified way and allow insecurities and doubt to take over your mind when your relationship hits a rough patch, you're going to be in trouble.

Written by Leslie Braswell

I've met a few women, who after time, become resentful and bitter because their husband or boyfriend is failing to meet their expectations. They ultimately become disappointed, and soon the relationship begins to unravel. The fact is, without realizing it, you may have become too dependent on someone else meeting your needs. Unknowingly you relied on another person for your happiness. When all the time, you had the power to meet all your needs right at your disposal. A woman who recognizes her value understands true happiness doesn't just come from one source. She doesn't put all her eggs in one basket. She doesn't become happy and then hands a person the power to determine whether she will continue to be happy or not. She never loses the remote control to her happiness. She keeps that power firmly in her own hands.

When you do start to think about what a man is not giving you, ask if he is even capable of providing it? He may not be. He may be working hard, focusing on achieving goals of his own. He may be doing the best he can just to keep his head above water. He may need your emotional support. He may need you to be self-sufficient.

Men abandon ship when women are too insecure, clingy, and unsure of themselves because they know how much overtime they will have to put in. Aim to be a self-sufficient woman who doesn't depend on validation from others to make her feel good enough. Have a life, something to do that is independent of Mr. Right. All you need to feel good is knowing you are doing the best you can with what God gave you to work with.

Stop trying to convince Mr. Ex to come back in your life and stop working so hard to impress Mr. Right to like you. The fact is when you stop trying to convince, that's when he'll take a double look your way. If a man doesn't want to be in your life, view it as his loss, *not yours.* When one door closes, another will open. Keep opening doors until you meet the man who meets your expectations without having to work hard at all.

The best man for you will love you regardless of how well you are performing. Stop getting frustrated with a man who isn't meeting your list of requirements. It's possible he's not ready for a woman like you. It's possible he doesn't have it to give. It's possible he's incapable of meeting all your needs. And why would you want to settle for less than the best?

Have you ever stopped to think that if Mr. Ex walked out of your life, maybe he did so for a reason? Perhaps it's part of a bigger plan for you. Perhaps there is someone better right around the corner. Through writing relationship books, I can't tell you how many women have written to me so heartbroken and discouraged. They thought they would never find love again. And then someone better than they could have ever imagined came into their lives. A few months later, I see engagement pictures, wedding pictures, or receive an invitation to their wedding. I'm so thrilled for them I could break out into the ugly cry.

If you have a history of dating the wrong men, you are the only one who can make a change. You've heard the old saying, "If you run with dogs, you're gonna get fleas." Stop running with dogs! If you know you're dating the dysfunctional bad boys who will never settle down, stop wasting your time on the impossible and start dating the possible. Start looking for someone deserving and appreciative of your love and affection.

Learn and live by the simple principle, to never depend on anyone for peace, happiness, encouragement, reassurance, or support. Your self-esteem, your self-worth, and how you value yourself won't take a direct hit when someone is not providing it to you. Don't misunderstand me; I want you to find a man who will give you compliments every day. I want you to have someone who makes you a priority in his life. But if you're not receiving that affirmation, I want you to be more than okay. If a man isn't telling you, you are beautiful, tell yourself, "I am beautiful." You can give yourself the encouragement you need every day. Before you leave your house, each morning say, "I am beautiful." "I am confident." "I am kind." "I am loving." "I am a great catch." "I am amazing." "A man would be so lucky to have me." When you build yourself up, nobody can tear you down. From this day forward, have a new expectation from any man you invite into your life. Expect a man to encourage you. Expect a man to be complimentary. Expect him to build you up. Expect him to make you a priority.

After all, he's lucky to have you.

A Recap of the Bitch's Break Up Rules

1. Silence is golden, use it.
2. Hide your crazy side.
3. Don't seek closure.
4. Don't express your love or anger.
5. Don't beg, plead, or bargain.
6. Don't fake an illness for sympathy.
7. If you break no contact, forgive yourself and start over.
8. Change his ringtone.
9. Change your screen saver.
10. Clean house and return anything that belongs to him.
11. Give him something to miss.
12. Strive to be the woman he fell in love with, only better.
13. Don't compete with other women.
14. Don't compare yourself to other women.
15. Don't obsess about his new love interest.
16. Be a catch.
17. Don't have ex-sex until he's giving you everything you want.
18. Don't stay in relationship limbo.
19. Know when to walk away.
20. Don't live bitter, live better.
21. Love yourself first.

A Woman's Only Flaw
Author Unknown

"When God created Woman, he was working late on the sixth day. An Angel came by and asked, 'Why spend so much time on her?' The Lord answered, 'Have you seen all the specifications I have to meet to shape her?'" "'She must function in all kinds of situations. She must be able to embrace several kids at the same time, have a hug that can heal anything from a bruised knee to a broken heart. She must do all this with only two hands. She cures herself when sick and can work 18 hours a day.'"

"The Angel was impressed. 'Just two hands? Impossible! And this is the standard model?' The Angel came closer and touched the woman. 'But you have made her so soft, Lord.' 'She is soft,' said the Lord, 'but I have made her strong. You can't imagine what she can endure and overcome.'"

"'Can she think?' the Angel asked. The Lord answered, 'Not only can she think, but she can also reason and negotiate.' The Angel touched her cheeks. 'Lord, it seems this creation is leaking! You have put too many burdens on her.' 'She is not leaking. It is a tear,' the Lord corrected the Angel. 'What's it for?' asked the Angel. The Lord said, 'Tears are her way of expressing her grief, her doubts, her love, her loneliness, her suffering, and her pride.'"

"This made a big impression on the Angel. 'Lord, you are a genius. You thought of everything. A woman is indeed, marvelous.' The Lord said, 'Indeed she is. She has strength that amazes a man.

Bitch Up!

She can handle trouble and carry heavy burdens. She holds happiness, love, and opinions. 'She smiles when she feels like screaming. She sings when she feels like crying, cries when happy, and laughs when afraid. She fights for what she believes in.

'Her love is unconditional. Her heart is broken when a next-of-kin or a friend dies, but she finds strength to get on with life.

"The Angel asked, 'So she is a perfect being?' The Lord replied, 'No. She has just one drawback.' 'She often forgets what she is worth.'"

Written by Leslie Braswell

Must Reads for Every Woman

It's called a Breakup, Because It's Broken *Written by Greg Behrendt and Amiira Ruotola-Behrendt*

For Women Only: What You Need to Know About the Inner Lives of Men *Written by Shaunti Feldhahn*

Girl, Stop Apologizing: A Shame-Free Plan for Embracing and Achieving Your Goals *Written by Rachel Hollis*

The Rules: Time-Tested Secrets for Capturing the Heart of Mr. Right *Written by Ellen Fein and Sherrie Schneider*

He's Just Not That Into You: The No-Excuses Truth to Understanding Guys *Written by Greg Behrendt and Liz Tuccillo*

Act Like a Lady, Think Like a Man: What Men Really Think About Love, Relationships, Intimacy, and Commitment *Written by Steve Harvey*

The Power of the Pussy: Get What You Want From Men: Love, Respect, Commitment and More! *Written by Kara King*

Other Books by Leslie Braswell

Ignore the Guy, Get the Guy
The Art of No Contact
A Woman's Survival Guide to Mastering a Breakup and Taking Back Her Power

How to Be the Girl Who Gets the Guy
How Confident and Self-Assured Women Handle Dating with Class and Sass

Do you have a story you would like to share? I would love to read about it.   You can contact me by sending an email to leslieannbraswell@gmail.com

Thank you for reading my book. I hope if you have a friend who needs reassurance, you will dust it off the bookshelf and share it with them.

Wishing you the best in everything,

Leslie Braswell

The End.

Printed in Great Britain
by Amazon

69918457R00071